Oktoberfest Cookbook

Julia Skowronek

Oktoberfest Cookbook

With photographs by
Brigitte Sporrer

Contents

A festival of opposites

What is it that makes Oktoberfest so fascinating and appealing? To find the answer, take a walk across the festival ground in Munich, ideally in the early afternoon when the autumn sun is shining and the crowds are still manageable. There, you will see groups of revellers who couldn't be more diverse, from young girls in brightly coloured mini dirndl dresses and teenage boys wearing hats shaped like beer mugs, to people in fancy dress and older locals in their traditional Bavarian attire. Have a peek inside the Hofbräu beer tent to find most of the visitors from Australia, North America, and New Zealand, enjoying the party atmosphere from the afternoon on. Whichever of the 14 large beer tents you choose: by the early evening, in every one of them people will be standing up on the benches, dancing, singing, and celebrating together.

Many and varied

Outside, the aromas of roast chicken, fish grilled on a skewer ("steckerlfisch"), roasted almonds, and candy floss will hint at the variety of food on offer. Stalls offer the fair's famous gingerbread hearts with their tender messages to the incurably romantic, others invite people to test their luck at classic funfair games. In the beer garden in front of the Fischer-Vroni tent, the relaxed atmosphere is perfect for a break from the hustle and bustle. Here, you might meet older married couples sitting in the sun, enjoying a beer and some skewer fish. They have probably been Oktoberfest regulars for over 40 years. In the background, resounding shrieks from the fearless visitors to the huge range of funfair rides mixes with brass bands and pop music from the beer tents, and the laughter and chatter of passers-by.

This may sound like a rather odd mix of short-lived trends and noisy, wild parties on the one hand, and traditional heritage on the other – but the Bavarians have seen it many times. "Passt scho!", they say, which means "It's all fine!" Since its beginnings, the largest folk fair in the world has been innovative and modern, yet at the same time visitors can experience traditional values, the glory of the past, and a relaxed and welcoming atmosphere.

Food paradise

Sometimes even local visitors are surprised at the range of food Oktoberfest offers beyond the classic roast chicken. The menus of both the large and the increasingly popular smaller beer tents, countless food stalls, and traditional restaurants offer a fantastic selection of Bavarian specialities. The food ranges from roast ox to fish sandwiches, from game to vegan dishes, from ham hock to fruit dipped in chocolate. Somewhere among these many choices you will discover your personal Oktoberfest favourite.

Inspired by this variety, we have gathered together the tastiest, most popular, and most traditional Bavarian Oktoberfest recipes in this book. Most of them are fairly straightforward in terms of ingredients and preparation. Use this book however you please: let it serve as your culinary tour guide while enjoying yourself at the festival. Once you have discovered your favourite beer tent and enjoyed the food and drink on the menu, you might want to cook your favourite dish at home and relive the memories of your visit. Maybe you prefer to avoid the hustle and bustle of the real thing and instead have your own Oktoberfest party. Choose from a mouth-watering selection of recipes and serve an authentic Bavarian feast to your friends and family. How about a "brotzeit" platter of sausage and cheese or a hearty soup, a juicy roast, and a homemade dessert? Don't forget to have a generous mug of German beer with the food – it will bring the taste and atmosphere of Oktoberfest even closer to you. Prost!

From royal wedding to the world's largest folk fair

The largest folk fair in the world has its roots in a jubilant royal wedding. On October 12, 1810, Crown Prince Ludwig, later King Ludwig I of Bavaria, married Princess Therese. The festival lasted for five days, and the young kingdom seized the opportunity to show off its greatness. Munich was filled with festival events, parades of men-at-arms, food and drink, musicians, and many other attractions. At the city gates, a horse race topped the bill on a field named in honour of the bride. It is this location that Oktoberfest is nicknamed after: the "Wiesn" – short for Theresienwiese, or Therese's meadow. The fair was so well received that it was soon decided to hold it annually. The horse races quickly faced competition from a growing variety of other attractions. First came carousels and giant swings, followed by amusements such as roller coasters and haunted houses, variety shows, curiosity cabinets, shooting stands, and games of chance. But even then, almost 200 years ago, what ultimately drew the locals to the Theresienwiese was the beer – more specifically, the Munich beer. As is still the case today, the rule was that only traditional Munich breweries were allowed to serve the specially brewed festival beer. Soon, even more visitors flocked to the fairgrounds. Towards the end of the 19th century, to cope with the crowds, the festival landlords and breweries set up the first giant tents. Michael Schottenhamel was the first of them, opening his tent in 1867 behind the King's tent. One by one, tents replaced the many small beer stalls. Today, Oktoberfest is still officially opened in the Schottenhamel tent by Munich's mayor, who taps the first barrel of beer and famously calls out "O'zapft is'!", which means "It is tapped!"

History of the fair

1810 The marriage of the Bavarian Crown Prince Ludwig and Therese von Sachsen-Hildburghausen is celebrated with a folk fair.

1818 Beer is served for the first time.

1835 On the occasion of his silver wedding anniversary, King Ludwig I holds a parade of people in historic traditional costumes. This is the precursor of today's traditional costume parade.

1850 The Bavaria – a gigantic statue on the heights to the west of Theresienwiese – is unveiled. Towering over the festival grounds, she symbolizes the Bavarian state.

1872 The start of Oktoberfest is brought forward to September due to better weather.

1880 The Oktoberfest site is electrified: around 400 restaurants, beer tents, and fair stalls now shine beneath the glow of electric lights.

1919 The first swing carousel, the "Kettenflieger Kalb", begins operating.

1950 For the first time, Oktoberfest is opened with the tapping ritual by the Mayor of Munich, Thomas Wimmer.

2010 Oktoberfest celebrates its 200th anniversary. A separated part of Theresienwiese is reserved for traditional festival tents and old-fashioned rides. The so-called "Old Fair" has since become a permanent feature of Oktoberfest.

Snacks and soups

Brotzeit platter with cheese,
cold meats, radish, and more

This handsomely arranged platter (or "brotzeit") of cold meats, cheese, and spreads, is the perfect start to an Oktoberfest evening. It is typcially accompanied by pretzels and, of course, a refreshing beer.

Serves 4 · Prep time: 30 minutes

For the platter
1 Daikon, or mooli, radish
bunch of radishes
4 dry-cured
    landjäger sausages
100g (3½oz) smoked
    ham, sliced
100g (3½oz) Emmental
    cheese, sliced
2 tbsp chopped chives
salt and freshly ground
    black pepper

For the Camembert spread
200g (7oz) Camembert cheese
200g (7oz) cream cheese, such
    as ricotta or cottage cheese
1 tbsp paprika
2 red onions
handful of salted pretzel sticks

For the radish spread
bunch of radishes
400g (14oz) cream cheese,
    such as ricotta or
    cottage cheese
squeeze of fresh lemon juice

For the rocket spread
2 handfuls of rocket leaves
400g (14oz) cream cheese,
    such as ricotta or
    cottage cheese
squeeze of fresh lemon juice

1   To prepare the platter, slice the Daikon radish very thinly, or use a spiralizer if you have one. Keeping the radishes bunched together, wash them thoroughly and leave to one side to drain. Cut the sausages in half.

2   To make the Camembert spread, break the Camembert cheese into small pieces with a fork. Add the cream cheese and combine. Season the spread with salt, pepper, and paprika. Peel the onions, slice into rings, and set aside.

3   To make the radish spread, coarsely chop the radishes. Stir in the cream cheese and season with salt, pepper, and lemon juice.

4   To make the rocket spread, coarsely chop the rocket leaves. Add the cream cheese to the rocket, combine well, and season the spread with salt, pepper, and lemon juice.

5   Arrange the slices of Daikon radish in the centre of a large wooden serving platter. Place the bunched radishes, landjäger sausages, sliced ham, Emmental cheese, and the three spreads around the radish. Garnish the Camembert spread with the onion rings and salted pretzel sticks. Scatter chopped chives over the entire platter and serve with salt and pepper on the side. Freshly-baked pretzel pastries (see p.113), and crusty bread go very well with this dish.

Tip: This platter can be varied to taste. For example, you can include any kind of dry-cured or cooked sausage, home-made liver sausage (see p.15), dill pickles, cold slices of roast suckling pig (see p.47), boiled ham hocks (see p.44), Oktoberfest chicken (see p.74), or spelt patties (see p.94). Open sandwiches with chives are also delicious on a brotzeit platter. To make these, generously butter slices of crusty bread and press the buttered sides into a dish of chopped chives.

Homemade leberwurst

with nutmeg and marjoram

Why not try making "leberwurst" (liver sausage) at home? It's easier than you might think. Decorated with a Bavarian-style blue-and-white label, a jar of this spread makes the perfect gift to bring to any Oktoberfest party.

Makes 6 jars (200ml/7fl oz each) · Prep time: 1 hour · Cooking time: 2 hours · Keeps for 6 months

500g (1lb 2oz) pork belly
   with rind
500g (1lb 2oz) pork neck, leg,
   or shoulder
500g (1lb 2oz) pork liver
salt and freshly ground
   black pepper
2 onions
1 tbsp vegetable oil
2 pinches of grated nutmeg
1 tbsp dried marjoram

You will also need
a meat mincer
6 sterilized jars, each holding
   200ml (7fl oz), and sterilized
   screw-top or self-sealing lids
   to match

1 Coarsely chop the pork belly, neck, and liver. Cover the liver and put it in the fridge. In a large pan, bring a generous amount of salted water to the boil. Place the pieces of pork in the water, reduce the heat, and cook for about 1 hour or until tender. Remove the meat with a slotted spoon, reserve the broth, and leave both to cool.

2 Peel the onions and chop them coarsely. Heat the oil in a frying pan, add the onions, and sauté until they are soft and translucent. Remove from the heat and leave to cool.

3 Using a fine grinder plate (4mm/³⁄₁₆in), put the liver, cooked pork, and fried onions through a meat mincer. Repeat. Pour 200ml (7fl oz) of the reserved broth over the liver sausage mixture and mix thoroughly. Season the mixture liberally with salt, pepper, nutmeg, and marjoram. Fill the sterilized jars, packing each no more than three-quarters full, and seal with the sterilized lids.

4 Fill a large pan with enough water to cover the jars. Bring the water to a rolling boil, then gently lower the jars into the water. Reduce the heat and boil for 1 hour at about 80°C (180°F). Alternatively, use a regular canner or pressure canner, and follow the manufacturers instructions. Remove the jars from the water and leave to cool. Serve the liver sausage as part of a Brotzeit platter (see p.12).

Tip: *You can vary the liver sausage recipe to taste. For example, try adding 2 stewed cubed apples, or 1 tablespoon of chopped flat-leaf parsley and 1 tablespoon of chopped chives, or 3 tablespoons of cooked cranberries to the sausage mixture. Another delicious variation is to substitute 2 tablespoons of coarsely chopped pistachios for the marjoram.*

Mixed salad

with deep-fried Camembert

This dish is a simple, yet delicious marriage of fresh, crunchy lettuce leaves and crisp fried cheese – a real Oktoberfest treat. No wonder this salad has so many fans.

Serves 4 · Prep time: 40 minutes

For the salad
1 apple
handful of cherry tomatoes
bunch of radishes
2 carrots
4 handfuls of mixed
    lettuce leaves
salt and freshly ground
    black pepper
3 tbsp vinegar
4 tbsp vegetable oil

For the fried Camembert
4 Camembert cheeses
    (150g/5½oz each)
3 eggs
2 tbsp flour breadcrumbs,
    for coating
oil, for deep-frying
4 tbsp lingonberry or
    cranberry compôte
    (from a jar), to serve
1 freshly baked pretzel,
    to serve

1   To make the salad, cut the apple into 8 pieces and remove the core. Slice the apple pieces, leaving the peel on. Cut the cherry tomatoes in half and slice the radishes. Peel and coarsely grate the carrots. Add the apple, tomatoes, radishes and carrots to the lettuce leaves in a large bowl, and toss.

2   Combine the salt, pepper, vinegar, and oil to make a dressing. Set aside until ready to serve.

3   To make the deep-fried Camembert, cut each cheese into quarters. Whisk the eggs in a shallow bowl. Put the flour and breadcrumbs on separate plates.

4   Dredge each piece of Camembert in the flour and shake off the excess. Then dip each piece in the beaten eggs, and finally into the breadcrumbs. Be sure to press the cheese pieces firmly into the breadcrumbs and shake off any excess. Dip each cheese wedge into the egg and then into the breadcrumbs for a second time.

5   Heat a generous amount of oil in a pan. Working in batches, deep-fry the pieces of Camembert in hot oil for about 5 minutes or until they are crisp on the outside. Remove and drain on paper towels.

6   Add the dressing to the salad, toss, and divide between four plates. Working quickly, place 4 pieces each of fried Camembert on top of each serving. Serve with the compote and a freshly baked pretzel on the side.

Sausage salad – three ways

Serves 4 · Prep time: 20 minutes each

For the dressing
salt and freshly ground
  black pepper
4 tbsp sherry vinegar
4 tbsp dill pickle liquid (from a
  jar) or vegetable broth
4 tbsp vegetable oil

1 Combine the salt, pepper, vinegar, dill pickle liquid, and oil to make a dressing. Set aside until ready to serve.

Bavarian sausage salad

600g (1lb 5oz) cooked deli
  sausage, such as Regensburg,
  bierwurst, ham or turkey
  kiełbasa, or bologna sausage
4 dill pickles (from a jar)
2 red onions

1 Remove the sausage casings. Thinly slice the sausage and the dill pickles. Peel the onions and slice them into thin rings. Place all the ingredients in a serving bowl.

2 Drizzle the dressing over the sausage, pickles, and onions, and toss. Leave the salad to marinate for about 15 minutes before serving.

Swiss sausage salad

400g (14oz) leberkäse, or
  alternatively use cooked deli
  sausage such as bierwurst,
  mortadella, ham or turkey
  kiełbasa, or bologna sausage
200g (7oz) Emmental cheese
1 bunch of radishes

1 Cut the sausage and Emmental cheese into thin strips. Trim and wash the radishes, and wash the radish greens. Slice the radishes and coarsely chop the greens. Put the sausage, Emmental cheese, and radish slices in a serving bowl.

2 Drizzle the dressing over the salad and toss. Leave the salad to marinate for about 15 minutes. Add the radish greens, toss again, and serve immediately.

Black pudding and pork terrine salad

4 slices black pudding sausage
  (80g/3oz each)
8 slices pork terrine or brawn
  (40g/1½oz each)
2 onions
2 dill pickles (from a jar)

1 Arrange the slices of black pudding sausage and pork terrine on 4 plates and drizzle with the dressing. Leave to marinate for about 15 minutes.

2 Peel the onions and slice them into rings. Cut the pickles in half lengthways, make lengthway cuts into each half, and fan out. Top the slices of black pudding and pork terrine with the onion rings and pickle, and serve.

Trout fillets, freshly smoked

Smoking fish at home is really easy and very satisfying – just make sure your kitchen is well ventilated first. You can conjure up all kinds of new flavours each time using different types of sawdust, herbs, and spices.

Serves 4 · Prep time: 30 minutes

2 bay leaves
4 sprigs of rosemary
4 sprigs of thyme
4 trout fillets, about
  150g (5½oz) each,
  boneless, and skin on
salt and freshly ground
  black pepper
1 piece of fresh horseradish
  root, about 4cm (1½in) long

You will also need
1 large food-safe metal tin
  (such as a biscuit tin)
3 handfuls of smoking sawdust
a cake rack or metal steamer
  rack that fits inside the tin

1   Using a large knife, screwdriver, or can opener, punch several holes into the lid of the metal tin.

2   Sprinkle the sawdust over the bottom of the tin. Break up the bay leaf and stir it into the sawdust, along with the rosemary and thyme. Sit the rack on the sawdust.

3   Season the fish fillets with salt and pepper and arrange them side by side, skin side down, on the cake rack. Put the lid on the tin and place it on the hob. Heat the tin over a medium heat until smoke begins to rise from the holes, then smoke the trout for about 10 minutes.

4   Meanwhile, finely grate the horseradish. When the fish is smoked, open the tin and remove the fillets. Sprinkle the grated horseradish over the smoked trout and serve.

Tip: You can re-use the tin several times. After you have smoked the fish, wash the tin, dry it thoroughly, and store it in a plastic bag.

What to wear: traditional dress

Dressing up for Oktoberfest has long been a tradition. However, the meaning of "dressing up" has changed dramatically since the beginning of the festival in 1810. Lederhosen (leather shorts) or a dirndl (a traditional dress) are almost mandatory for today's visitor. The shorts were formerly the work clothes of farmers, while the dirndl was worn by maidservants and farmers' wives in the 19th century.

However, they haven't always been the traditional Oktoberfest outfit. At the beginning of the 20th century, citizens dressed in their best clothes for a day at the fair – men wore tuxedos and top-hats, women their best dresses. It wasn't until the 1960s that the idea of traditional costume and Oktoberfest came together, and at the beginning of the 21st century traditional dress has become the norm, even for visitors from around the world. A dirndl is not always a dirndl though, and sturdy leather shorts come in various lengths and qualities. So how do you dress properly for the fair? It may seem confusing, but if you follow a few basic rules, you won't go far wrong.

Traditional women's costume

Whatever your age or shape, every woman looks great in a dirndl, as it is designed to flatter the figure. The dress is always worn with an apron. Dirndls come in a variety of colours, cuts, and patterns today – flowers, stripes, checks, and more; there's a style for every taste. The ideal Oktoberfest dirndl falls just below the knee, although traditionalists prefer ankle-length skirts. You might also see mini-skirt dirndls at the fair. However, these are a recent invention and don't have much in common with the traditional dirndl. The essential undergarments are a blouse, usually white, and a special dirndl bra with three-quarter cups and widely spaced straps to reveal and emphasize the cleavage. The festival outfit is complemented by a matching

hairstyle. Braids and updos are especially popular. They can be quite tricky to create, and if you want to be on the safe side, have your hair braided or styled by a hairdresser. Finally, don't forget to bring along a warm jacket – a traditional one if you want your outfit to be entirely authentic – because you will feel the cold when you leave the beer tent.

Traditional men's costume

Men have a choice of leather shorts: they come in long, short, or knee-length styles, and a variety of materials. Depending on your budget and taste, you can choose from deerskin, mountain goat- or goatskin, as well as cowhide. Some have yellow, green, or white embroidery, and come with or without suspenders. Lederhosen should fit snugly and be comfortable to wear. Men with muscular calves tend to wear "loferl", or knitted calf warmers. If your legs are more slender, the regular traditional socks will look good on you. Lederhosen are worn with a Bavarian button-down chequered shirt and a matching jacket.

Jewellery and shoes

Women's traditional attire is typically complemented by modest silver jewellery, which is often decorated with rubies, mountain crystals, or pearls. Worn by both men and women, the "charivari" used to be a talisman for hunters and farmers. These short silver chains are adorned with small hunting trophies, lucky charms, precious stones, or coins. Women wear them on their dirndl bodice and men on the waist of their leather shorts. You can buy them in shops, but according to tradition, a charivari is either presented as a gift or inherited. Charms are added to it over time before it is eventually passed on to the next generation. Finally, the outfit is completed with matching shoes. Pumps or elegant shoes with reasonably high heels go best with a dirndl. They should be comfortable for several hours of dancing and celebrating, and sturdy enough to protect your feet from broken glass splinters on the floor – after all, not all of the beer mugs survive the festival. For men, the traditional "haferlschuh", with laces on the sides, go very well with leather shorts, but any pair of hiking shoes or boots will do perfectly well.

The bow code

The apron bow of a dirndl reveals what kind of relationship the wearer is in:

Bow on the left – single
Flirting is allowed or even encouraged when your bow is tied on your left. So if you aren't married, but are in a relationship, be careful where you tie your bow!

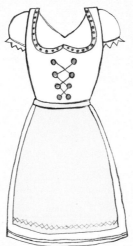

Bow at the back – widow
If people offer you their condolences for no obvious reason, you might want to check the position of your bow. If it's tied at the back, it is saying that you are a widow.

Bow on the right – taken
Traditionally, this style was only adopted by married women. However, anyone who wishes to avoid unwanted attention can take advantage of its message.

Gravlax sandwiches

with home-made cured salmon

The snack and fish stalls at the fair offer a huge range of fish sandwiches, but the "lachssemmel", or gravlax roll, remains a classic choice. Lots of food stalls actually use a cheaper fish, such as artificially coloured pollock, instead of salmon. The gravlax sandwiches in this recipe, however, are guaranteed to be topped with genuine home-cured salmon.

Serves 4 · Prep time: 40 minutes · Brining time: 12 hours

1 lemon
150g (5½oz) salt
150g (5½oz) sugar
½ tsp black peppercorns
1 salmon fillet, about
    600g (1lb 5oz), boneless,
    and skin on
2 large eggs
1 red onion
4 bread rolls
butter, for the bread
2 tbsp chopped dill
handful of salad leaves

1 Wash and slice the lemon. Mix the salt, sugar, and black peppercorns. Sprinkle half the seasoning mixture into a deep casserole dish and arrange half the lemon slices on top. Place the salmon fillet on top of the lemon, sprinkle over the remaining seasoning, and top with the remaining lemon slices. Cover the dish and leave in the fridge for 12 hours to brine.

2 Boil the eggs for about 8–10 minutes until hard-boiled. Rinse under cold running water, peel, and slice the eggs. Peel the onion and slice into rings. Cut the bread rolls in half and butter the cut sides.

3 Remove the salmon from the brine, wash it in cold water, and pat dry. Then sprinkle the dill evenly over the salmon. Cut the fillet into very thin slices.

4 Arrange a few salad leaves on the cut side of the top half of each roll. Place several slices of gravlax on the bottom half. Add a layer of onion rings and then a layer of sliced egg on top of the salmon, cover with the top half of the roll, and serve immediately.

Tip: Another classic dish is the pickled (or Bismarck) herring sandwich. To make it, slice 1 onion into rings and cut 2 dill pickles from a jar into slices. Cut open 4 bread rolls and layer each bottom half with 1 pickled herring fillet, some of the onion slices, and some of the dill pickle. Cover with the top halves of the rolls and enjoy!

Matjes fillets
in a creamy apple-and-yogurt sauce

Chicken, ham hocks, sausages, roast duck... with so much meat on offer, fresh soused herrings, or "matjes", are a welcome change. One of the Oktoberfest beer tents has even made fish dishes its speciality, notably the classic "steckerlfisch", or fish grilled on a skewer.

1 onion
2 dill pickles (from a jar)
1 apple
salt and freshly ground
  black pepper
4 tbsp mayonnaise
300g (10½oz) low fat,
  plain yogurt
4 tbsp dill pickle liquid
  (from a jar)
2 tbsp chopped dill
4–8 soused herring fillets;
  alternatively, mildly
  seasoned, pickled herring
  fillets from a jar, such as
  wine-marinated herring

Serves 4 · Prep time: 20 minutes

1 Peel the onion and slice it into rings. Slice the dill pickles. Cut the apple into 8 pieces. Remove the core and slice the apple, leaving the peel on.

2 Bring a large pan of salted water to the boil. Blanch the onion slices, and set aside to drain.

3 Mix together the mayonnaise, yogurt, and dill pickle liquid. Stir in the onion, pickles, sliced apple, and dill. Season the sauce with salt and pepper to taste.

4 Rinse the herring fillets in cold water and pat them dry with paper towels. Divide the sauce between four plates and arrange a double herring fillet on each plate. Parslied potatoes (see p.103) go well with this dish.

Tip: Fancy some colour in this dish? Adding red beetroot will turn the sauce bright pink. Cook 2 medium beetroots for about 45 minutes until tender, and leave to cool. Peel the beetroots, cut them into slices, and then stir into the apple-and-yogurt sauce. If you are in a hurry, use sliced beetroots from a jar.

Autumnal squash soup
with pumpkin seed oil

Sitting outside in the afternoon, enjoying the autumn sun, is a wonderful thing to do during Oktoberfest. With the cold season just around the corner, a warming dish is perfect for the occasion – such as this lovely squash soup.

Serves 4 · Prep time: 40 minutes

1 onion
1 piece of celeriac, about 55g
   (2oz)
1 small carrot, about 55g (2oz)
½ leek, about 90g (3oz)
1 parsnip, about 90g (3oz)
handful of flat-leaf parsley
1 Hokkaido squash (red kuri
   squash), about 750g
   (1lb 10½oz)
2 tbsp vegetable oil
800ml (1¼ pints)
   vegetable broth
1 bay leaf
4 sprigs of thyme
2 tbsp pumpkin seeds
200ml (7fl oz) double cream
salt and freshly ground
   black pepper
pinch of grated nutmeg
2 tbsp pumpkin seed oil,
   for drizzling

1   Peel and coarsely dice the onion. Coarsely chop the celeriac, carrots, leek, parsnip, and parsley. Wash the squash, cut it in half, and scrape out and discard the seeds. Cut the squash into large pieces.

2   Heat the oil in a large pan, add the onion, and sauté. Stir in the remaining vegetables, the parsley, and the squash, and continue to sauté for about 5 minutes. Pour in the vegetable broth. Add the bay leaf and thyme. Bring everything to the boil, then reduce the heat and simmer for about 20 minutes or until the vegetables are tender.

3   Meanwhile, dry-fry the pumpkin seeds for about 3 minutes in a frying pan, stirring constantly. Set aside.

4   Remove the thyme and bay leaf from the soup. Using a hand-held blender, purée the soup in the pan. Then return it to the boil, stir in the cream, and season with salt, pepper, and nutmeg.

5   Serve in soup bowls, with pumpkin seeds scattered over the top and a drizzle of pumpkin seed oil.

A guide to the beer tents

Standing on a bench, singing and celebrating with thousands of other people in one of the huge Oktoberfest tents is a truly amazing experience. There are 14 large tents to choose from, and in all of them the landlords serve beer from one of the traditional Munich breweries. Atmosphere, decoration, visitors, size, and food menus are different in every tent, so choose wisely where you would like to celebrate. There is a number of smaller beer tents, too. If you prefer not to spend the evening in a huge crowd, there are plenty of places all over the fairgrounds.

Party essentials

Despite their differences, the large tents have one thing in common, the music. Brass and party bands get the crowds going all day long. In the afternoon, you will hear mostly traditional Bavarian brass music. But at about 6 o'clock in the evening, as soon as the roast chicken and ox has been consumed, the tempo increases, the breaks between songs become shorter and less frequent, and the top Oktoberfest hits – well-known German party songs or classic rock, pop, and country hits – are played one after the other, until everyone is on their feet. However, the evening's overall success depends less on the music, than on the service. A good waiter or waitress is the manager of the tables at Oktoberfest. The waiters will keep an eye on their guests, be quick to bring the next round, and won't show

if they are stressed. Although the myth of the cranky and feisty Oktoberfest waiter persists, today, friendly and attentive service is highly valued at Oktoberfest, and your waiters will be nice to you if you are nice to them. Respect and good manners are called for at the fair just like anywhere else.

Getting into the tents

Oktoberfest attracts millions of people every year. This means that on weekends, and also some weekdays, the beer tents are often closed due to overcrowding. The rules are strict: only when one visitor leaves, can another enter. Unfortunately there is no special trick, convincing argument, plea, insult, or charm offensive that will presuade the bouncers to let you in – they've heard and seen it all before. So, make you you are at your tent of choice early, or be prepared to spend a lot of time waiting to go in.

If you want to be sure of getting a table in a tent, you should reserve it early. You can only reserve tables for about ten people, with no single seats on offer. From January onwards, tent landlords accept reservations for the current year. Contact and booking information can usually be found on the website of the respective tent. Processing the requests is often a lengthy process, so you will have to be patient. Table reservations are free, but tied to a minimum spend. Usually, you are asked to purchase coupons for two litres of beer and half a roast

chicken per person, to be paid in advance. That said, the costs can add up to significantly more than this, so check well in advance before you book your table.

Choosing the right tent

So, which tent is the right one for me? Here are a few guidelines to help you decide. If you are a fan of traditional Bavarian "gemütlichkeit", which roughly means a feeling of coziness and friendliness, head to the Augustiner, Armbrustschützen, Ochsenbraterei, or Winzerer Fähndl tent. By contrast, the wildest and most international parties await you in the Hofbräu and Löwenbräu tents. Here you will meet the greatest number of overseas visitors, for example from Australia, New Zealand, and North America. The crowd is a bit younger in the Schottenhamel and Schützen tents, and also in the Hacker tent (nicknamed "Bavarian Heaven" for its ceiling, which is painted with clouds and stars). The Bräurosl tent is the place to be for the gay community. Your choice of tent can also be influenced by culinary considerations. All those who crave a serving of freshly roasted ox on a spit should make their way to the Ochsenbraterei tent. Anyone who would rather eat grilled fish on a skewer are in the right place in Fischer-Vroni's tent or its outdoor beer garden. In the opulently decorated Marstall tent, which features a large Champagne bar, the atmosphere is much more dignified. Here, and in Kuffler's Weinzelt tent, which is the place to go for wine afficionados, the majority of the crowd is over 30. At Käfer's gourmet tent you can mingle with VIPs, the rich, and the beautiful.

Those who want to avoid the hustle and bustle of the main festival ground and the large tents, and who would rather sit than stand on a bench, will feel more comfortable in the Herzkasperl and Tradition tents located in the separate "Old Fair" area. With a historic atmosphere and music played by bands from the Munich music scene, they are very charming places away from the crowds. Be aware, though, that there is a small admission fee to the "Old Fair" area, and it occasionally is closed off if it becomes too busy.

Hearty goulash soup
with Oktoberfest beer

Oktoberfest is undoubtedly fun, but it can get a bit chilly outside, as summer draws to an end. If the autumn sun fails to warm you up, try a bowl of this hearty beef soup instead.

Serves 4 · Prep time: 35 minutes · Cooking time: 1 hour

500g (1lb 2oz) onions
oil, for frying
500g (1lb 2oz) boneless beef
  (such as neck, leg, or shin),
  cut into small cubes
1 tbsp tomato purée
1 tbsp paprika
250ml (9fl oz)
  Oktoberfest beer, or other
  German-style amber lager
salt
1 tsp dried marjoram
1 tsp caraway seeds
zest of 1 lemon
500g (1lb 2oz) waxy potatoes,
  such as Charlotte
2 red peppers
fresh marjoram leaves,
  to garnish

1   Peel the onions and dice them finely. In a large pan, heat up a little oil. Add the diced onions and sauté. Add the cubes of beef and fry for about 10 minutes or until the beef juices have completely evaporated.

2   Stir in the tomato paste and sprinkle the paprika over the meat. Pour in the beer to deglaze the pan, then add 750ml (1¼ pints) of water. Season with salt, marjoram, caraway seeds, and lemon zest, and bring to the boil. Now reduce the heat and simmer the soup for about 1 hour, stirring now and then.

3   Meanwhile, peel the potatoes. Remove the seeds and stems from the red peppers. Coarsely dice the potatoes and peppers. Add the diced potatoes to the pan about 15 minutes before the end of the cooking time, and the diced pepper about 5 minutes before the end.

4   Serve the goulash soup in shallow bowls, sprinkled with fresh marjoram, to taste. Crusty bread goes well with this dish.

Clear chicken soup

with noodles and vegetables

Hot chicken soup with plenty of meat and noodles is a perfect dish to warm you up, and is bound to make you feel happy and content. This soup serves 6 people as a starter or 4 as a main course.

Serves 4–6 · Prep time: 40 minutes · Cooking time: 1 hour

1 chicken, about
  1.2kg (2½lb)
salt
1 piece of celeriac, about
  125g (4½oz)
1 carrot, about 125g (4½oz)
1 leek, about 180g (6oz)
1 parsnip, about 180g (6oz)
handful of flat-leaf parsley
½ tsp black peppercorns
1 bay leaf
150g (5½oz) dried
  soup noodles
2 tbsp chopped parsley,
  to garnish

1 Bring a large pan of salted water to the boil and add the chicken (it should be just covered with water). Return the water to a rolling boil and boil the chicken for about 5 minutes. Skim off any scum that rises to the surface. Coarsely chop half the celeriac, carrot, leek, parsnip, and all the parsley. Add the chopped vegetables to the chicken, along with the parsley, peppercorns, and bay leaf. Simmer over a low heat for about 50 minutes. Check the pan occasionally to make sure the chicken is always covered with liquid, and add more water as needed.

2 Meanwhile, dice the remaining vegetables. Cook the dried soup noodles in boiling salted water according to the instructions on the package. They should be soft but still have bite. Drain the noodles in a sieve and rinse under cold running water.

3 Remove the chicken from the broth and leave to cool. Pour the broth through a fine mesh sieve into another pan, then return the broth to the boil.

4 Remove the skin from the cooked chicken. Take the meat off the bone and cut it into bite-size pieces.

5 Add the diced vegetables to the broth and cook until al dente. Just before serving, add the cooked chicken pieces and the noodles to the broth to warm them through. Ladle into soup bowls, garnish with chopped parsley, and serve.

Liver dumpling soup
with chopped chives

This hearty soup is a classic starter for an Oktoberfest meal. When eating at the fair, it's best to have soups only at lunchtime – in the evening, when waiters and waitresses have to balance their trays as they move through the packed beer tent, soup bowls often arrive at your table only half full!

Serves 4 · Prep time: 40 minutes

For the liver dumplings
4 rolls of day-old bread
250ml (9fl oz) milk
200g (7oz) beef liver
1 onion
1 tbsp unsalted butter
2 large eggs
2 tbsp chopped
  flat-leaf parsley
salt and freshly ground
  black pepper
pinch of grated nutmeg
1 tsp dried marjoram
1 tsp grated lemon zest

To serve
1 litre (1¾ pints) beef broth
  (from boiled beef, see p.57)
2 tbsp chopped chives

1 To make the liver dumplings, thinly slice the rolls and place the slices in a bowl. Boil the milk, pour it over the sliced rolls, and mix thoroughly. Leave to soak for about 15 minutes.

2 Meanwhile, chop the liver into small pieces and purée. Peel the onion and dice it finely. Melt the butter in a frying pan, add the onion, and sauté.

3 Thoroughly combine the liver, onion, eggs, and parsley with the bread-and-milk mixture. Season with salt, pepper, nutmeg, marjoram, and lemon zest.

4 In a shallow pan, bring salted water to the boil. Form dumplings the size of golf balls from the liver mixture and place them in the boiling water. Reduce the heat and poach the liver dumplings for about 15 minutes.

5 Meanwhile, bring the beef broth to the boil. Using a slotted spoon, remove the liver dumplings from the salted water and lower them into the hot broth. Ladle the broth and dumplings into soup bowls, sprinkle with chopped chives, and serve.

Tip: The liver dumplings can also be served with sauerkraut (see p.44), to make an excellent main course.

Leek and potato soup
with pretzel croûtons

Today's soup of the day is this creamy leek and potato soup with crunchy fried pretzel croûtons. Enjoy!

Serves 4 · Prep time: 40 minutes

For the soup
2 leeks, about 180g (6oz) each
1 onion
600g (1lb 5oz) floury potatoes,
   such as Maris Piper
1 piece of celeriac, about
   125g (4½oz)
2 tbsp vegetable oil
1 bay leaf
800ml (1¼ pints)
   vegetable stock
200ml (7fl oz) double cream
salt and freshly ground
   black pepper
pinch of grated nutmeg

For the croûtons
2 day-old baked pretzels
2 tbsp unsalted butter

1 To make the soup, cut off the white part of one of the leeks and set aside the green part. Peel the onion, potatoes, and celeriac. Coarsely chop the vegetables and the white part of the leek. Thinly slice the entire second leek and the green green end of the first leek into rings, and set aside.

2 Heat the oil in a large pan, add the onion, and sauté. Add the potatoes, celeriac, leeks, and bay leaf and sauté for a few minutes. Pour in the vegetable broth and simmer over a low heat for about 15 minutes. Remove the bay leaf and purée the soup in the pan using a hand-held blender. Return to the boil, stir in the double cream, and season the soup with salt, pepper, and nutmeg, to taste.

3 Bring a pan of salted water to the boil. Add the sliced leeks and blanch, then set aside.

4 To make the croûtons, slice the pretzels. Melt the butter in a frying pan, add the slices, and fry until golden brown, stirring constantly.

5 Stir the blanched leeks into the soup to warm them. Ladle out the soup into shallow bowls, scatter pretzel croûtons over the top, and serve.

Tip: Pale creamy soups – such as this – will have an especially lovely colour if you only use light-coloured vegetables such as onion, celeriac, parsnip, and the white part of the leek.

Mains

Pork schnitzel cordon bleu

This crisp and juicy pork dish is a variation of the classic Wiener schnitzel. Filled with ham and cheese, it is a great and filling main, best served with potato salad.

8 thinly cut boneless pork
  loin chops, each about
  80g (3oz)
salt and freshly ground
  black pepper
4 slices cooked ham
4 slices Emmental cheese
2 large eggs
2 tbsp flour
breadcrumbs, for coating
vegetable oil, for frying
1 lemon, to serve

You will also need
meat tenderizer
toothpicks

Makes 4 portions · Prep time: 30 minutes

1　Using a meat tenderizer, pound each pork chop into a thin schnitzel and season with salt and pepper. Lay out 4 schnitzels side by side on a cutting board. Top each with 1 slice of ham, 1 slice of Emmental cheese, and a second schnitzel. Use toothpicks to pin together the two schnitzels and their filling.

2　Whisk the eggs in a shallow bowl. Put the flour and breadcrumbs on two separate plates.

3　Dip both sides of each schnitzel into the flour and shake off the excess. Now dip both sides of the meat into the egg, and finally into the breadcrumbs. Press each schnitzel lightly into the breadcrumbs and shake off the excess.

4　In one large, or two small, frying pans, heat a generous amount of oil, enough so the schnitzels will float in the oil. Put the schnitzels in the hot oil and fry them on one side. As you are frying, gently shake the frying pan back and forth so that the oil flows over the schnitzels. When they are golden brown underneath, turn the schnitzels over and reduce the heat. Fry until golden brown, then drain on paper towels.

5　Cut the lemon into quarters and serve the pork schnitzels with the lemon slices. Potato and endive salad (see p.110) goes well with this dish.

Variation: If you like your schnitzel even richer, fill each of them with 1 slice of prosciutto and 1 slice of blue-veined cheese, such as Gorgonzola.

Boiled ham hocks
on a bed of sauerkraut

In Munich and Bavaria salt-cured meat is called "surfleisch," and if you would like to eat boiled ham hocks at Oktoberfest, you would order "surhaxn". Elsewhere in Germany, they are commonly known as "eisbein".

Serves 4 · Prep time: 20 minutes · Cooking time: 1 hour 30 minutes

For the ham hocks
salt
4 ham hocks (also called pork
  knuckles), pickled in brine
1 piece of celeriac, about
  55g (2oz)
1 small carrot, about 55g (2oz)
½ leek, about 90g (3oz)
1 parsnip, about 90g (3oz)
handful of flat-leaf parsley
½ tsp black peppercorns
1 bay leaf

For the sauerkraut
1 onion
1 tbsp vegetable oil
500g (1lb 2oz) sauerkraut
300ml (10fl oz) pork or
  vegetable stock
½ tsp black peppercorns
½ tsp juniper berries
1 clove
1 bay leaf
pinch of sugar
salt

1 In a large pan, bring salted water to the boil, enough to just cover the pickled hocks. Add the hocks and return the water to a rolling boil, then cook the meat for about 5 minutes. Using a slotted spoon, skim off any scum that rises to the surface. Reduce the heat and simmer the hocks for about 1 hour 30 minutes. Make sure the meat is always covered with liquid, and add more water as needed.

2 Coarsely chop the celeriac, carrot, leek, parsnip, and parsley. After half the cooking time – about 45 minutes – add the vegetables and parsley, the peppercorns, and the bay leaf to the pot. Cook the hocks for another 45 minutes.

3 Meanwhile, prepare the sauerkraut. Peel the onion and slice it into rings. Heat the oil in a pot, add the onion, and sauté. Add the sauerkraut and pour in the stock. Add the black peppercorns, juniper berries, clove, bay leaf, and sugar. Season the sauerkraut with salt to taste, and simmer over a low heat for about 20 minutes.

4 Remove the hocks from the stock. Strain the stock through a fine mesh sieve and reserve to use in another dish, such as sauerkraut. Arrange the ham hocks and the sauerkraut on a platter and serve. Classic mashed potatoes or parslied potatoes (see p.103) go very well with this dish.

Tip: If you prefer, you can cook the ham hocks and the sauerkraut in one pot. Sauté the onion and add the sauerkraut, celeriac, carrot, leek, parsley, and seasonings, as described above. Place the ham hocks on the sauerkraut and add enough water to completely cover them. Cook for about 90 minutes. Top up the water as needed to ensure the hocks are always covered with liquid.

Roast suckling pig
with onion stuffing

This delicious rolled pork loin roast comes with an aromatic onion stuffing and an intensely flavoured beer-based sauce. If you prefer to keep it simple, leave out the stuffing – the meat is just as wonderful on its own.

Serves 6 · Prep time: 40 minutes · Cooking time: 2 hours

3 onions
1 tbsp vegetable oil
1 tsp dried marjoram
1.2kg (2½lb) loin of suckling
  pig, boneless, with skin
  and belly fat on (order
  from the butcher)
1 tbsp mustard
salt and freshly ground
  black pepper
1 tsp caraway seeds
1 piece of celeriac, about
  55g (2oz)
1 small carrot, about 55g (2oz)
½ leek, about 90g (3oz)
1 parsnip, about 90g (3oz)
handful of flat-leaf parsley
500ml (16fl oz) Oktoberfest
  beer or other German-style
  amber lager

You will also need
kitchen twine

1 To make the filling, peel 2 of the onions and slice them into rings. Heat the oil in a frying pan and add the onions. Fry them for about 5 minutes, turning often. Season with the marjoram, remove from the stove, and leave to cool.

2 Preheat the oven to 180°C (350°F/Gas 4). Lay the pork loin flat on a cutting board, skin side down. Spread the mustard over the loin, and season it with salt and pepper. Distribute the fried onions evenly over the meat. Starting at the thickest end, roll up the loin, and tie it with kitchen twine.

3 Season the pork loin all over with the salt, pepper, and caraway seeds, and place in a roasting tin. Peel the remaining onion. Coarsely dice the onion, celeriac, carrots, leek, and parsnip. Chop the parsley. Add the diced vegetables to the roasting tin and pour in 250ml (9fl oz) of water.

4 Place the pork in the middle of the oven and roast it for about 2 hours. Baste the meat with the juices every 15 minutes. If the skin turns too dark or doesn't brown enough, reduce or increase the oven temperature. Add a little more water as necessary. Towards the end of the roasting time, pour the beer over the pork.

5 Remove the pork loin from the roasting tin and keep warm. Pour the sauce through a fine mesh sieve into a pan and set aside briefly, then carefully spoon off all the fat that has risen to the surface. Return the gravy to the boil.

6 Carve the roast into thick slices and serve with the gravy. Potato dumplings (see p.104) and Bavarian cabbage (see p.99) are classic sides for this dish.

Tip: If suckling pig is not commonly sold in your area, you can also make a classic pork roast by following this recipe, but instead of loin of suckling pig, use 1kg (2.2lb) of pork shoulder, skin on (ask your butcher to score the skin for you), season as described above, and roast the pork for about 2 hours. The roast will serve four.

It's all about the sausage

Feel like having sausage today? But which one? These are the five most common types of Bavarian sausage sold at Oktoberfest. Weißwurst, by the way, is a genuine Munich speciality, traditionally eaten before midday.

Weißwurst

A mild-tasting "white sausage" made from veal and parsley (centre). Put 2 white sausages per person into boiling salted water, reduce the heat immediately, and poach the sausages gently for about 15 minutes. To remove the casing before eating, cut open the sausage lengthways and remove the sausage meat. Traditionally, the meat is sucked out, but this only works if the sausage is very soft – and if you are experienced. As an accompaniment, pretzels and sweet mustard are a must.

Wollwurst

The name of this sausage (bottom right) translates to "wool sausage" because it doesn't have a casing. Dip 1–2 sausages per person in milk, then fry them on each side in hot oil for about 10 minutes until browned. Meat gravy, such as roast suckling pork gravy (see p.47), and potato salad (see p.110) or classic mashed potatoes (see p.103) go well with this type of sausage.

Milzwurst

A poached sausage (top right) made with pieces of spleen, hence the name "spleen sausage". For each person, fry 1–2 finger-thick slices of milzwurst in hot oil for about 10 minutes until browned on each side. Add a little gravy to taste. Another delicious way of preparing them is to dip the slices in breadcrumbs and fry them just like pork schnitzel (see p.43). Serve with potato and endive salad (see p.110) and remoulade sauce (see p.78), to taste.

Schweins- würstel

A sausage made from coarsely minced pork (top left). Cook 4 "pork sausages" per person on the grill or in a frying pan in hot oil on each side for about 10 minutes until crispy. These sausages are best served with sauerkraut (see p.44) and medium-hot mustard.

Leberkäse

Another Bavarian speciality which misleadingly translates to "liver cheese", this finely-minced sausage meat (bottom left) is baked in the oven. Serve 1 thick slice of leberkäse per person, ideally freshly baked. You can also fry slices of leberkäse in hot oil on each side for about 5 minutes until browned. Fried eggs, fried onions (see p.82), potato salad (see p.110), and sweet mustard – always a must in Bavaria – go well with this.

A showcase for Munich beer

Oktoberfest has always been a festival by Munich citizens for Munich citizens. This is why only six traditional local breweries are allowed to serve beer at the fair. Even today, breweries outside the city borders are not granted a licence to serve at the fair.

Oktoberfest beer

Oktoberfest beer is brewed exclusively for the festival by the local breweries. It is a bottom-fermented beer, just like the classic Munich Helles, but has a higher alcohol content of about six per cent by volume, due to its higher wort (fermented malt) content. Every Oktoberfest beer has its own character, of course, but generally the beer served at the fair has a slightly bitter and malty taste. It's less highly carbonated than other beers, is very easy to drink, and is also very strong at the same time. The beer is brewed according to the Munich "purity law" of 1487, which was extended to the whole state of Bavaria in 1516. It states that only barley (or malted barley), hops, and water are allowed to be used for brewing. The yeast, which is necessary for fermentation, was added to the list of permitted ingredients much later.

The "mass" (pronounced with a short "uh" sound, as in "bus") is both a measuring unit for the beer and the name of the vessel it is served in. The pottery mugs used at earlier Oktoberfests have long ago been replaced by glass mugs. One benefit of this is that it makes it easier for them to check if their beer mugs have been "badly poured" – in other words, not filled up to the standard measure line.

The six traditional Munich breweries

The Augustiner brewery is the oldest Munich brewery. As early as 1328 a brewery existed in the Augustiner monastery on Neuhauser Gasse. The monastery pub was very popular with the locals. In the early 19th century the monastery and its brewery were secularized, and in 1817, the brewery was passed into private hands. Of the "big six", Augustiner is the only brewery that is still family-owned and still stores the beer in traditional wooden barrels. This time-honoured brew is served in the Augustiner tent, the Fischer-Vroni tent, and in the Herzkasperl tent in the historic part of Oktoberfest – the "Old Fair."

The story of the Hacker-Pschorr brewery began in 1417 on Sendlinger Straße, where the restaurant Altes Hackerhaus still exists today. When Therese Hacker and Joseph Pschorr married in 1793, a brewing dynasty was founded. Their sons ran Hacker and Pschorr as separate breweries for many years, until they were merged in 1972. At 5.8 per cent by volume, the alcohol content of Hacker-Pschorr is the lowest of all the Oktoberfest beers. It is served in the Hacker tent, in the Pschorr Bräurosl tent, and in the Herzkasperl tent at the "Old Fair".

The history of the Löwenbräu brewery dates back to the late 14th century. It became one of the large breweries in 19th-century Munich, and a public company as early as 1872, setting up its headquarters on Nymphenburger Straße. Löwenbräu then merged with Spaten and Franziskaner breweries, and has, since 2004, belonged to the AB InBev Group, which merged with Anheuser Busch in 2008 to become the world's largest brewery company. Löwenbräu Oktoberfest beer is served in the Löwenbräu and Schützen tents.

Paulaner beer can be traced back to 1634, when it was brewed in the monastery of the Pauline monks on Neuhauser Straße. This makes it the "youngest" of all Munich beers. Paulaner has also become well-known for the "starkbieranstich", the annual tapping of the first barrel of bock beer at the political satire festival hosted by the brewery in March. The golden Paulaner ale is served in the Armbrustschützen, Winzerer Fähndl, and Käfer's gourmet tents.

Spaten brewery was first mentioned in a document in 1397 and has changed hands many times since then. In 1807, it was purchased by the Royal Court Brewer, Gabriel Sedlmayer. His initials can still be seen on the company logo, a white spade on a red background, designed in 1884. Until the 1890s, Spaten was Munich's largest brewery. Today, just like Löwenbräu, it belongs to AB InBev. The legacy of Spaten beer is strong: Oktoberfest is officially opened in the Schottenhamel tent with the tapping of a barrel of Spaten. It is served in the Marstall and Ochsenbraterei tents.

Hofbräu was founded in 1589 during the reign of the Bavarian Duke Wilhelm V. The brewery was located on Platzl, near Marienplatz, where the world-famous Hofbräuhaus still is today. The brewery has been owned by the state of Bavaria since the 19th century. In 1896, the brewery moved to Haidhausen, and a restaurant was built in its former place. In 1988 the brewery needed even more space and moved again, this time to Riem.

With an alcohol content of 6.3 per cent, Hofbräu is the strongest of the Oktoberfest beers and is served in the Hofbräu tent.

As in most walks of life, beer gets a little more expensive every year. The Oktoberfest beer price is set in advance and can vary slightly, depending on the venue. In 1971, a mass of Oktoberfest beer cost between 2.50 and 2.95 German Marks (about £1). In 2002, when the Euro was introduced, the price rose to 6.30 Euro (about £4.50). In 2014, the price crept over the 10 Euro (about £7.20) mark for the first time. However, this doesn't seem to affect the enjoyment of millions of visitors, or the popularity of Oktoberfest beer.

Oktoberfest food: from roast to strudel

Oktoberfest is rightly famous for its delicious beer from the breweries of Munich, which is consumed in huge quantities. However, beer is best served with a hearty Bavarian meal, and in this respect Oktoberfest has a lot to offer. A good, fair landlord is not just someone who taps the most beer, has their tent under control, and employs the quickest waiters. He or she must also make sure that people enjoy the food sent out to the tables on huge trays. After all, there is plenty of competition among tents, stalls, and restaurants!

Delicious Oktoberfest classics

The most popular dishes are roast chicken, pork sausages, ham hocks, duck, various roasted meats, and cheese spaetzle. These dishes are served everywhere across the festival, but some favourites are only available in certain tents.

Sometimes the name of the establishment gives it away. At Ochsenbraterei (oxen grill), ox are roasted on a spit – in fact, about 100 of them are consumed during Oktoberfest. The first ever Oktoberfest ox was roasted on a specially constructed spit in 1881. Just like in the old days, the name and weight of the animal turning on the spit is written on a large board above the grill. An entire ox feeds many hungry visitors, and the Ochsenbraterei menu boasts a huge variety of meat dishes.

On the other hand, anyone who likes "steckerlfisch" – fish grilled on a skewer – cannot ignore another long-time institution, the Fischer-Vroni tent. The menu includes mackerel, char, salmon, trout, whitebait, and sea bass. The fish are spitted on skewers, lined up in a long row, and grilled over an open fire. The best side to accompany grilled fish is a crisp, fresh pretzel – and of course a fresh mug of beer.

For those looking for culinary variety, a visit to the smaller festival tents will prove very rewarding. In the Kalbsbraterei, Munich Knödelei, or Wildstuben tents, for example, or in one of several time-honoured establishments serving roast chicken and duck, the owners develop their own special dishes and take pride in the reputation they have built for themselves. However, it isn't just meat-lovers who will find happiness at Oktoberfest. As more and more people are choosing a vegetarian or vegan diet, the food concession owners have adapted to suit them. For some time now, a growing range of vegetarian dishes has been sold in the tents, such as creamy

wild mushroom stew (see p.89), cheese spaetzle, and spinach spaetzle (see p.82). Those who don't eat eggs and dairy no longer have to bring their own food: several landlords offer dishes such as soy medallions, vegan cheese spaetzle, or vegetable-and-potato burgers. Nobody is allowed to leave Oktoberfest on an empty stomach!

Sweet treats

Don't forget to top off your meal with a sweet treat. (And who's counting calories at Oktoberfest anyway?) Strudel, kaiserschmarrn (see p.120 and p.124) or doughnuts are among the many irresistible temptations. And for those who like simple desserts, many stalls

offer chocolate-dipped fruit, toffee apples, candy floss, nougat, or bags of roasted almonds to warm your hands. You will find classic Oktoberfest sweets to cook at home starting on p.114.

Anyone who wants to enjoy the culinary side of Oktoberfest in peace and quiet should go to the fair at lunchtime on a weekday. This is the quietest time of the week, and it's much easier to find a seat. It's easier on your wallet, too – on weekdays between 10am and 3pm, many establishments offer reasonably priced lunch menus, which change daily. On sunny days, there is even a genuine beer garden atmosphere on the festival ground during lunchtime and in the early afternoon.

On average, each year fair-goers consume ...

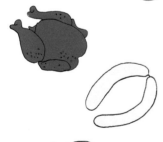

500,000 roast chickens

250,000 pork sausages

80,000 ham hocks

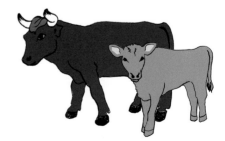

110 oxen and 90 calves

Stuffed breast of veal

This Bavarian classic is ideal for serving to a large number of guests. As it is a main and side dish in one, you won't need to cook anything else.

Serves 6 · Prep time: 50 minutes · Cooking time: 2 hours

1 portion of bread dumplings (see p.104)
200g (7oz) cooked ham
zest of ½ organic lemon
1 piece of celeriac, about 55g (2oz)
1 small carrot, about 55g (2oz)
½ leek, about 90g (3oz)
1 parsnip, about 90g (3oz)
handful of flat-leaf parsley
1.5kg (3.3lb) trimmed boneless breast of veal, ready for stuffing (ask your butcher to make a pouch in the meat)
salt and freshly ground black pepper
2 tbsp vegetable oil
1 bay leaf

You will also need
kitchen twine

1 Prepare the bread dumpling mixture as described on page 104. Dice the ham. Add the ham and the lemon zest to the dumpling mixture and combine. Coarsely dice the celeriac, carrot, leek, and parsnip. Chop the parsley.

2 Preheat the oven to 180°C (350°F/Gas 4). Season the veal inside and out with salt and pepper. Stuff the dumpling mixture into the pouch and sew it up with kitchen twine.

3 Heat the oil in a roasting pan, add the breast of veal and brown it on all sides. Add the vegetables, parsley, and bay leaf, and pour in about 700ml (1¼ pints) of water. Roast the veal in the middle of the oven for about 2 hours, basting the meat now and then with the roasting juices. Add a little more water as necessary.

4 Remove the veal from the oven and the roasting pan, and keep warm. Pour the roasting juices through a fine mesh sieve into a pan and return to the boil. Carve the stuffed breast into thick slices and serve with the juices. A mixed salad goes well with this.

Boiled beef
with fresh horseradish

This Bavarian classic is not just popular during Oktoberfest. Boiled beef, called "tellerfleisch" in Bavaria, can be prepared fairly effortlessly at home, and the resulting broth can be served as a delicious soup.

Serves 4 · Prep time: 40 minutes · Cooking time: 2 hours

To make the boiled beef
salt
1kg (2.2lb) boneless beef
  (chuck or shoulder)
1 piece of celeriac, about
  125g (4½oz)
1 carrot, about 125g (4½oz)
1 leek, about 180g (6oz)
1 parsnip, about 180g (6oz)
handful of flat-leaf parsley
½ tsp black peppercorns
1 bay leaf
2 tbsp chopped chives

To serve
4 tbsp freshly grated
  horseradish
4 dill pickles (from a jar)

1 In a large pan, bring enough salted water to the boil to just cover the beef. Add the beef and cook at a rolling boil for about 5 minutes. Using a slotted spoon, skim off any scum that rises to the surface. Reduce the heat and simmer for about 2 hours. Add water as necessary to ensure that the meat is always covered with liquid.

2 Meanwhile, coarsely chop half of the vegetables and all the parsley. About 45 minutes before the end of the cooking time, add the vegetables, parsley, peppercorns, and bay leaf to the pan. Cut the remaining vegetables into bite-size pieces and set aside.

3 Remove the boiled beef from the pan and keep warm. Pour the broth through a fine mesh sieve into a second pot and return it to the boil. Add the reserved chopped vegetables to the pan and simmer in the broth until al dente.

4 Carve the beef into finger-thick slices. Arrange the slices of beef and vegetables on soup plates and pour over a ladle of broth. Sprinkle with chives and serve with horseradish and dill pickles on the side.

Tip: Make two dishes from one: from the remaining broth you can make an exceptional beef soup in no time at all. Cook 150g (5½oz) of dried noodles in boiling salted water, following the instructions on the package. Drain the noodles in a sieve and reheat them in the broth along with 4 tablespoons of cubed boiled beef. Sprinkle with 2 tablespoons of chopped chives and serve.

Tender sauerbraten

in red wine sauce

Tender, braised beef and tasty gravy always make a great meal. A side dish of pan-fried or boiled potatoes complement it perfectly.

Serves 4 · Prep time: 30 minutes · Cooking time: 2 hours · Marinating time: 3 days

1 onion
1 piece of celeriac, about 55g (2oz)
1 small carrot, about 55g (2oz)
½ leek, about 90g (3oz)
1 parsnip, about 90g (3oz)
handful of flat-leaf parsley
1kg (2.2lb) boneless silverside beef
5 black peppercorns, coarsely crushed
1 tsp allspice
4 juniper berries, coarsely crushed
2 cloves
2 bay leaves
1 tsp mustard seeds
500ml (16fl oz) red wine
125ml (4½fl oz) red wine vinegar
salt and freshly ground black pepper
2 tbsp vegetable oil
2 tbsp flour
1 tbsp tomato purée

1 Peel the onion. Coarsely dice the onion, celeriac, carrot, leek, and parsnip. Chop the parsley. Put the beef, chopped vegetables, parsley, and spices in a bowl. Add the red wine and red wine vinegar, cover the meat, and leave to marinate in the fridge for at least 3 days, turning it occasionally. Make sure the meat is always covered with liquid, and add more wine if needed.

2 Preheat the oven to 180°C (350°F/Gas 4). Remove the meat from the marinade and season it all over with salt and pepper. Strain the marinade through a sieve set over a bowl and reserve the liquid. Set aside the vegetables and spices left in the sieve.

3 Heat the oil in a roasting pan. Add the beef, brown it on all sides, and remove. Add the vegetables and spices. Sauté, then sprinkle with flour and stir in the tomato purée. Now pour in the reserved marinade, bring it to the boil, and return the meat to the pan. Place the roast in the middle of the oven and braise for about 2 hours, turning it now and then. Add a little water if necessary.

4 Remove the roast from the roasting pan and keep warm. Pour the roasting juices through a fine mesh sieve into a pan and briefly return to the boil. Cut the sauerbraten into finger-thick slices and arrange on four plates with the sauce. Spaetzle (see tip, p.82) and red cabbage (see p.99) make good sides for this dish.

Beef roulades
stuffed with dill pickles and bacon

Roulades are a classic Oktoberfest lunch. Why not enjoy an alcohol-free beer, or a "radler" (shandy) with them? Afterwards, you could either return to work... or just stay where you are if you're having a good time!

Serves 4 · Prep time: 50 minutes · Cooking time: 1 hour

100g (3½oz) smoked
  back bacon
2 dill pickles (from the jar)
3 onions
3 tbsp vegetable oil
salt and freshly ground
  black pepper
1 tsp dried marjoram
4 pieces of boneless silverside
  beef, about 200g (7oz) each,
  pounded to 6mm (¼in)
2 tbsp mustard
1 piece of celeriac, about
  55g (2oz)
1 small carrot, about
  55g (2oz)
½ leek, about 90g (3oz)
1 parsnip, about 90g (3oz)
handful of flat-leaf parsley
2 tbsp flour
1 tbsp tomato purée
150ml (5fl oz) red wine
1 bay leaf

You will also need
toothpicks

1 Cut the bacon and dill pickles into strips. Peel 2 onions and slice them into rings. In a frying pan, heat 1 tablespoon of oil and fry the bacon until crisp. Remove and drain on kitchen paper. Add the onion rings to the pan and fry for about 5 minutes. Season with salt, pepper, and marjoram, and set aside to cool.

2 Lay the pieces of beef side by side on a chopping board, spread each piece with mustard, and season with salt and pepper. Distribute the bacon, onions, and pickles over the pieces of meat, leaving a clear edge about the width of a finger all the way around each piece. Turn in the edges, roll up the roulades, and secure with toothpicks.

3 Peel the remaining onion. Coarsely dice the onion, celeriac, carrot, leek, and parsnip. Chop the parsley. In a large pan, heat the remaining oil, add the roulades, and brown them on all sides. Remove from the pan and set aside. Now add the onion and diced vegetables to the pan and sauté. Sprinkle over the flour and stir in the tomato purée, then add the red wine to deglaze the pan and add 750ml (1¼ pints) of water. Add the parsley and bay leaf, and bring to the boil. Return the roulades to the pan and simmer in the sauce over a low heat for about 1 hour, stirring occasionally. Season with salt and pepper. If the sauce reduces too much while the roulades are cooking, add a little more water.

4 Lift the roulades out of the pan and keep warm. Pour the sauce through a fine mesh sieve into a second pan and return briefly to the boil. Serve the roulades with the sauce and either classic mashed potatoes (see p.103) or spaetzle (see tip, p.82).

Tip: To find out if the meat is cooked, insert a skewer into the roulades (or the roast) at the end of the cooking time. If it goes straight through, the meat is cooked. If not, cook for another 15 minutes and test again.

Lung stew

Lung stew might seem an unusual dish, but if you've never tried it before, you're in for a real treat. Served with bread dumplings, it is an affordable and very popular Oktoberfest lunch.

Serves 4 · Prep time: 45 minutes · Marinating time: 8 hours

5 black peppercorns, crushed
1 tsp allspice
4 juniper berries, crushed
2 bay leaves
1 tsp mustard seeds
½ lemon
800ml (1¼ pints)
   vegetable stock
150ml (5fl oz) sherry vinegar
salt and freshly ground
   black pepper
1 pinch of sugar
500g (1lb 2oz) cooked lungs
   (from calf, cow, or pig),
   cut into strips
1 onion
2 tbsp clarified
   unsalted butter or ghee
2 tbsp flour
2 tbsp chopped parsley,
   to garnish

You will also need
kitchen twine

1 Put the spices in a paper coffee filter or a piece of cheesecloth and tie with kitchen twine. Cut the lemon into slices. Pour the vegetable stock into a pot, add the vinegar, spice sachet, and lemon slices, and bring to the boil. Season with salt, pepper, and sugar, remove from the stove, and set aside to cool.

2 Place the cooked lungs into the cooled liquid, cover, and marinate them in the fridge for at least 8 hours.

3 Strain the lungs through a sieve set over a bowl, reserving the marinade. Discard the spice sachet and the lemon slices.

4 Peel the onion and dice it finely. Heat the clarified butter in a large pan, add the onion, and sauté until golden brown. Dust with flour and fry until the onion is dark-gold in colour, stirring constantly. Pour in all the marinade and continue stirring while it comes to the boil. Then reduce the heat and simmer the sauce for about 10 minutes, stirring frequently.

5 Add the marinated lungs to the sauce and simmer over a low heat for about 10 minutes. Serve the lung stew in shallow bowls, sprinkled with parsley. Bread dumplings (see p.104) also work with this dish.

Tip: Cooked lungs sliced into thin strips are sold in almost every butcher shop in Bavaria. If they're not available in your area, see if your butcher can order raw lungs, also known as lights, and cook them yourself. Wash the lungs, then peel and coarsely chop 1 onion. Bring a large pan of salted water to the boil, add the lungs, the onion, and 1 or 2 bay leaves, and simmer for about 2 hours, or until the lungs are tender. Remove from the pan, remove any veins and gristle, and slice into very thin strips. The lungs are now ready to be used.

Venison stew

in a juniper and red wine sauce

With the venison hunting season in full swing in Bavaria during the Oktoberfest period, there are so many delicious game dishes on offer at the festival, it's hard to make a choice.

Serves 4 · Prep time: 40 minutes · Cooking time: 1 hour

1 onion
1 piece of celeriac, about
   55g (2oz)
1 small carrot, about
   55g (2oz)
½ leek, about 90g (3oz)
1 parsnip, about 90g (3oz)
handful of flat-leaf parsley
1kg (2.2lb) stewing venison
salt and freshly ground
   black pepper
2 tbsp vegetable oil
2 tbsp flour
1 tbsp tomato purée
200ml (7fl oz) red wine
1 tsp juniper berries
1 bay leaf
2 cloves
½ tsp black peppercorns
200g (7oz) sour cream,
   to serve

1 Peel the onion. Coarsely dice the onion, celeriac, carrot, leek, and parsnip. Chop the parsley. Season the meat with salt and pepper.

2 Heat the oil in a large pan, add the meat, and brown it on all sides. Remove from the pan and set aside. Add the chopped onion and celeriac, carrot, leek, and parsnip to the pan and sauté in the remaining oil. Dust the vegetables with the flour and stir in the tomato purée. Add the red wine to deglaze the pan and add 1 litre (1¾ pints) of water. Put the meat, parsley, juniper berries, bay leaf, cloves, and black peppercorns in the pan. Bring everything to the boil, reduce the heat, and simmer for about 1 hour, stirring now and then. If the liquid reduces too much, add a little more water.

3 Using a slotted spoon and tongs, lift the meat out of the sauce and set aside. Pour the sauce through a fine mesh sieve into a second pan and bring to the boil. Add the meat to the sauce to reheat.

4 Serve each portion of stew with a dollop of sour cream on top. Spaetzle (see tip, p.82) and red cabbage (see p.99) go well with venison stew.

Tip: Poached pear halves filled with cranberry sauce make an excellent fruity side for venison stew. Peel 2 pears, cut them in half, and remove the cores. Fill a pan with enough white wine or water to cover the pears, add 1 tablespoon of sugar and ½ cinnamon stick, and bring to the boil. Add the pears and simmer over a low heat for about 10 minutes. Remove the pears with a slotted spoon and fill each pear half with 1 tablespoon of cranberry or lingonberry compote (from the jar). If you are in a hurry, use canned pear halves.

Braised lamb shanks
on root vegetables

Slowly braised lamb shanks are a lighter alternative to the rich roast ham hocks on offer. Freshly poured Oktoberfest beer goes very well with this.

Serves 4 · Prep time: 35 minutes · Cooking time: 1 hour

4 lamb shanks
   (300g/10½oz each)
salt and freshly ground
   black pepper
3 tbsp vegetable oil
1 tbsp tomato purée
150ml (5fl oz) red wine
1 bay leaf
2 sprigs of rosemary
4 sprigs of thyme
250g (9oz) shallots
4 carrots
4 parsnips

1 Season the lamb shanks with salt and pepper. Heat 2 tablespoons of oil in a large pan and brown the shanks on all sides, then remove them from the pan. Add the tomato purée to the pan and fry briefly. Pour in the red wine to deglaze the pan and add 750ml (1¼ pints) of water. Add the bay leaf, rosemary, and thyme, and bring everything to the boil. Now return the lamb shanks to the pot and simmer over a low heat for about 1 hour, stirring now and then. Season the sauce with salt and pepper.

2 Meanwhile, peel the shallots, but leave them whole. Cut the carrots and parsnips into thick slices.

3 Heat the remaining oil in a large frying pan. Add the vegetables and sauté them for about 5 minutes. About 15 minutes before the end of the cooking time, add the root vegetables to the lamb shanks and cook until tender. To deglaze the frying pan in which you sautéed the vegetables, add 120ml (4fl oz) of water and bring to the boil. Add the liquid to the lamb shanks.

4 Serve the lamb shanks with the root vegetables and the sauce. Dumplings (see p.104) are also good with this, or a simple bread roll.

Two turbulent weeks: Oktoberfest highlights

Oktoberfest usually lasts 16 days, starting on the first Saturday after September 15th and coming to an end on the first Sunday in October. If the last Sunday happens to be the 1st or 2nd of October, the festival is extended to the 3rd of October – German Unity Day – and then lasts up to 18 days. Most visitors attend the fair on each of the three weekends, as not everyone can, or wants to, take time off. If you can visit during the week, though, you will find it's less busy than at the weekends – when the tents have to be closed due to overcrowding.

The Grand Entry

The festival is openend with a spectacular parade that both tourists and Munich residents enjoy watching: the so-called Grand Entry of the Oktoberfest Landlords and Breweries. Early on Saturday morning, the streets of the route are closed off and at 11am, the parade sets off. Decorated brewery wagons pulled by teams of dray horses garlanded with flowers and bunting, tent landlords, waiters, market vendors, and showmen wend their way through the city centre. Passing by crowds of spectators along the route, they make their way to the festival ground at Theresienwiese via Josephspitalstraße, Sonnenstraße, and Schwanthalerstraße.

The parade is led by the Münchner Kindl (meaning "Munich child"), a young woman dressed in a black and yellow monk's habit, riding on horseback. She is the symbol of Munich, representing the figure shown on the city's coat of arms. She is followed by first the mayor's, and finally the tent landlords' and their staff's carriages. Waving to the crowd, holding beer mugs, the tent staff sit on the wagons next to the decorated wooden beer barrels, with the sound of jingling harness bells and brass music announcing their arrival at the fair.

In years gone by, the festival beer was delivered on horse-drawn wagons, and the tradition continues today, much to the pleasure of visitors. However, the beer is usually stored in steel containers, or transported, as in the Hacker tent, through a circular underground "beer pipeline". Only in the Augustiner-serving tents is it still served from large wooden barrels.

"O'zapft is'!"

As soon as the parade is over, a wooden barrel becomes the centre of attention. At exactly midday, surrounded by the press and celebrities, the mayor of Munich taps the first barrel of Oktoberfest beer in the Schottenhamel tent by driving a tap into it with a mallet. The following announcement "O'zapft is'!" – "It's tapped!" – officially starts Oktoberfest. The number of blows it takes the mayor to tap the barrel is always the subject of much speculation and scrutiny: the fewer taps, the more in command the mayor appears, which is why the heads of the city hall are always happy to receive a bit of training from a barrel tapping expert. It is tradition for the first beer to be given to the Bavarian state premier, and any political differences are set aside for the day.

Folk costumes and riflemen

The following day, the first Oktoberfest Sunday, is all about tradition, when the huge Costume and Riflemen's Procession makes its way to Theresienwiese. Thousands watch and cheer as folk and sport-shooting groups,

brass and marching bands, and standard-bearers march through the city, accompanied by decorated carriages and horse-drawn brewery wagons. The parade starts at the Maximilian II monument near the Isar river, progresses along Maximilianstraße through the city centre, and finishes at Esperantoplatz in front of the festival ground. About 9,000 participants proudly show their original and often highly elaborate folk costumes from their home regions – not only Bavaria, but from all over Germany, other parts of Europe, and even North America. There are also historic costumes on show, ranging from the Middle Ages to Art Nouveau, interspersed with military groups and famous figures from local history and myths, such as the Schmied von Kochel (the blacksmith of Kochel) or the 17th century sculptor Erasmus Grasser.

The parade has a long tradition: first held in 1835 in honour of the silver wedding anniversary of Ludwig I and Therese von Bayern, it has been staged at every Oktoberfest since 1948, and has been an integral part of the festival and a visitors' favourite ever since.

Visitors from the south

A party of a different kind takes off towards the end of the second festival week: the so-called Italian weekend. Every year, thousands of Italians come to Munich for the "festival della birra" (festival of beer). Italians make up the largest group of Oktoberfest visitors – about a fifth of the crowd. The party atmosphere is more heated than usual during this weekend, and newspapers even publish Oktoberfest maps in Italian. The citizens of Munich accept it: after all, the locals like to see Munich as "the northernmost city of Italy."

On the final evening of the festival, the waiters serve the last mugs of beer. Emotional closing ceremonies are held in each tent. Sparklers and sing-alongs transform these tents into very special festive places during the final minutes of the fair, and several visitors and waiting staff cry farewell tears. But there is one consolation: as this year's Oktoberfest comes to an end, there's always next year to look forward to!

Crispy duck
with apple and onion stuffing

Duck, like chicken, is usually roasted on a spit at Oktoberfest. However, at home it's better to slowly roast the bird in the oven. This way, you will be able to reserve the juices and use them to make delicious gravy.

Serves 4–6 · Prep time: 25 minutes · Cooking time: 2 hours

1 duck, about 2.5kg (5½lb)
salt and freshly ground
  black pepper
2 apples
4 onions
1 tsp dried marjoram
1 piece of celeriac, about
  55g (2oz)
1 small carrot, about
  55g (2oz)
½ leek, about 90g (3oz)
1 parsnip, about 90g (3oz)
handful of flat-leaf parsley
4 sprigs of mugwort

1 Preheat the oven to 180°C (350°F/Gas 4). Rinse the duck inside and out with cold water and pat dry. Season the duck inside and out with salt and pepper.

2 To make the filling, wash the apples, quarter them, and remove the cores. Peel 2 onions. Coarsely chop the apples and onions, mix together, and season with marjoram, salt, and pepper. Stuff the duck with the apple-and-onion mixture and place it in a roasting pan.

3 Add about 250ml (9fl oz) of water to the roasting tray and roast the duck in the middle of the preheated oven for about 2 hours. Baste the duck occasionally with the juices. Add a little more water as required. If the skin turns too dark or does not brown enough, reduce or increase the oven temperature.

4 Peel the remaining onions. Coarsely chop the onions, celeriac, carrot, leek, and parsnip. After about 1 hour of the cooking time, scatter the onions, vegetables, and the parsley and mugwort sprigs around the duck in the roasting pan.

5 At the end of the cooking time, remove the duck from the roasting pan and keep warm. Pour the sauce through a fine mesh sieve into a second pan and set aside for a few minutes. Then carefully skim off the fat that has risen to the surface and return the sauce to the boil.

6 Carve the duck into 4 to 6 portions and remove the filling. Serve with the sauce, dumplings (see p.104) and red cabbage (see p.99).

Bavarian chicken hash
and fresh vegetables

It is hard to believe, but sometimes there are leftovers at Oktoberfest. This delicious hash is great for making use of leftover meat, for example from a roast chicken.

Serves 4 · Prep time: 40 minutes · Cooling time: 1 hour

800g (1¾lb) waxy potatoes, such as Charlotte (or leftover boiled potatoes)
salt and freshly ground black pepper
500g (1lb 2oz) mixed vegetables (such as green beans, cauliflower, and carrots)
2 onions
1 roast chicken (see p.74)
2 tbsp vegetable oil
2 tbsp chopped parsley, to garnish

1 Boil the potatoes in salted water for about 20 minutes, or until cooked. Drain, let the steam evaporate briefly, and peel. Leave the potatoes to cool for about 1 hour, then cut them into slices.

2 In a second pan, bring salted water to the boil. Blanch the green beans for a few minutes until al dente. Then plunge them into ice water and drain in a sieve. Cut the cauliflower into small florets and slice the carrots. Peel the onions and slice into rings.

3 Remove the chicken meat from the bone and cut it into bite-sized pieces. Heat the oil in one large or two small frying pans. Add the potatoes, green beans, cauliflower, carrots, onions, and chicken pieces. Turning often, fry the chicken and vegetables over a high heat for about 10 minutes until golden brown.

4 Season with salt and pepper, sprinkle with parsley, and serve immediately.

Tip: *Hash, or "gröstl", is a classic Bavarian recipe for using up leftovers – to make it, use anything you like or whatever you happen to have in the fridge. Roast chicken can be substituted with roast pork, roast duck, roast beef, smoked bacon, or ham. And instead of boiled potatoes try potato dumplings, bread dumplings, or pretzel dumplings. Select fresh seasonal vegetables: leek, broccoli, red pepper, and celeriac all work well in this hash. Or leave out the vegetables entirely. If you feel like it, serve fried eggs with the hash, or whisk 2 or 3 eggs, pour them over the hash towards the end of the cooking time, and leave to set.*

Oktoberfest chicken

Eating chicken with your fingers is one of the simple pleasures at Oktoberfest. After all, the meat is much easier to pull apart without cutlery.

Serves 4 · Prep time: 15 minutes · Cooking time: 45 minutes

1 tbsp paprika
pinch of cayenne pepper
1 tsp curry powder
1 tsp sugar
salt and freshly ground
  black pepper
2 chickens
  (900g/2lb each)
handful of flat-leaf parsley
2 tbsp unsalted butter

You will also need
salt for the baking tray

1   Place an oven rack in the middle of the oven. Preheat the oven to 180°C (350°F/Gas 4). Sprinkle a layer of salt about 1cm (½in) thick on a baking or roasting tray. Place the tray on the next oven rack down.

2   Combine the paprika, cayenne pepper, curry powder, sugar, salt, and pepper in a small bowl. Rub the seasoning into the chickens, inside and out. Put 2 sprigs of parsley and 1 tablespoon of butter in each cavity.

3   Place the chickens directly on the oven rack above the baking or roasting tray. Roast the chickens for about 45 minutes, or until they are fully cooked and the skin is crispy.

4   Cut the chickens in half lengthways and then into individual portions. Serve with potato salad (see p.110), pretzel pastries (see p.113), or pretzels.

Tip: To make roast ham hocks, or "schweinshaxn", mix 1 teaspoon each of caraway seeds and paprika and add some salt and pepper to taste. Use the spice mix to liberally season 4 fresh (not smoked or pickled) pork hocks – ask the butcher to score the skin for you. Roast the hocks as described above for 90 minutes. About 30 minutes before they are done, baste the hocks with 250ml (9fl oz) of Oktoberfest beer. Serve with Bavarian cabbage (see p.99) or Bavarian cabbage slaw (see p.100).

Pan-fried char
with lemon-and-parsley butter

The Bavarians love this regional freshwater fish dredged in flour and pan-fried, with just a few simple ingredients.

4 whole char, about
  350g (¾lb) each
  (alternatively, use
  freshwater trout or salmon)
salt and freshly ground
  black pepper
flour, for dredging
oil, for frying
4 tbsp unsalted butter
2 tbsp chopped parsley
juice of 1 lemon
lemon wedges, to serve

Serves 4 · Prep time: 30 minutes

1 Rinse the char in cold water, pat them dry, and season inside and out with salt and pepper. Sprinkle flour on a large plate. Dredge the fish on both sides in the flour and shake off the excess.

2 Heat some oil in two large frying pans. Place 2 char in each pan, reduce the heat, and fry the fish on each side for about 5 minutes, basting them frequently with the hot oil.

3 Carefully drain off the oil. Melt the butter in the frying pans and carry on frying the fish, shaking the pans back and forth to make the butter foam. Add the parsley and lemon juice, and shake the pans again.

4 Lift the fish out of the frying pans and serve immediately, garnished with lemon wedges and accompanied by parslied potatoes (see p.103).

Tip: To make original "steckerlfisch" – skewer-grilled fish – on your home barbecue, use 1 whole cleaned and washed fish (such as char, trout, mackerel) per person, season to taste with salt and pepper, and stuff each fish with 1 sprig of thyme. Cook the fish on the hot grill for about 5 minutes on each side, or until done.

Beer battered fish
with remoulade sauce

Bavaria is a predominantly Catholic area, so it is customary to eat fish on Fridays. Tradition and the Church are closely linked: children are even baptised at Oktoberfest during an annual service held in one of the gigantic beer tents.

Serves 4 · Prep time: 50 minutes

For the remoulade sauce
2 dill pickles (from the jar)
1 tbsp capers (from the jar)
2 anchovy fillets
4 tbsp mayonnaise
150g (5½oz) plain yogurt
2 tbsp chopped
  flat-leaf parsley
salt and freshly ground
  black pepper

For the battered fish
4 fish fillets for deep-frying
  (such as cod, hake, haddock,
  or pollock)
juice of 1 lemon
150g (5½oz) flour
150ml (5fl oz)
  Oktoberfest beer, or other
  German-style amber lager
2 large eggs
oil, for deep frying
lemon wedges, to serve

1　To make the remoulade sauce, very finely chop the dill pickles, capers, and anchovies. In a bowl, stir together the mayonnaise, yogurt, dill pickles, capers, anchovies, and parsley. Season with salt and pepper and chill in the fridge until ready to serve.

2　To prepare the fish, rinse the fillets with cold water and pat dry. Drizzle with the lemon juice and season with salt and pepper.

3　Whisk the flour and beer together to make a thick batter, and season it with salt and pepper. Separate the eggs and stir the egg yolks into the batter. In a separate bowl, beat the egg whites until they form stiff peaks. Carefully fold the batter into the beaten egg whites.

4　Heat enough oil in a shallow pan for the fish to float when you fry them. One at a time, dip the fish fillets into the batter, allow any excess to drip off, and immediately lower the fish into the hot oil. Fry on each side for about 5 minutes until golden brown. Using a slotted spoon, lift the fillets out of the oil and drain on kitchen paper.

5　Cut the remaining lemon into wedges. Serve the fish immediately, with the remoulade sauce and lemon wedges on the side. Potato salad (see p.110) goes well with this.

Vegetarian and side dishes

Spinach spaetzle

with fried onions

Both spinach and cheese spaetzle are particularly popular with American Oktoberfest visitors. After all, this Swabian-Bavarian classic, with its layers of melted cheese, could be seen as a German version of Mac 'n' cheese!

Serves 4 · Prep time: 40 minutes

450g (1lb) chopped
  frozen spinach
salt and freshly ground
  black pepper
250g (9oz) plain flour
125g (4½oz) semolina
3 eggs
pinch of grated nutmeg
150g (5½oz) freshly grated
  Emmental cheese
2 onions
1 tbsp unsalted butter, plus
  more for the casserole dish

You will also need
a spaetzle maker

1 Defrost the spinach according to the instructions on the package. Preheat the oven to 180°C (350°F/Gas 4). Butter an ovenproof dish.

2 In a large pan, bring a generous amount of salted water to the boil. In a large bowl, combine the flour and semolina. Add the eggs and spinach, and season with salt, pepper, and nutmeg. Beat the mixture to make a thick batter that drips slowly off a wooden spoon. Continue beating vigorously for about 5 minutes, until small bubbles form.

3 Ladle a portion of batter into the spaetzle maker and grate the spaetzle straight into the boiling water. When the spaetzle float to the surface, remove them with a slotted spoon and drain briefly. Place a layer of spinach spaetzle in the casserole dish and top with a layer of grated cheese, then put the dish in the oven to keep warm. Carry on in this way until the dough and cheese are used up.

4 Peel the onions and slice into rings. Melt the butter in a frying pan and sauté the onions until golden brown. Top the spaetzle with the fried onions and serve immediately. A leafy green salad goes well with this dish.

Tip: For classic spaetzle, combine 250g (9oz) plain flour, 125g (4½oz) semolina, 4 eggs, salt, grated nutmeg, and 200ml (7fl oz) of cold water to make a batter, and cook as described above. To serve, cut 2 tablespoons of unsalted butter into small pieces and stir into the spaetzle. Both spaetzle dishes make excellent side dishes for sauerbraten (see p.58) and venison stew (see p.65), for example.

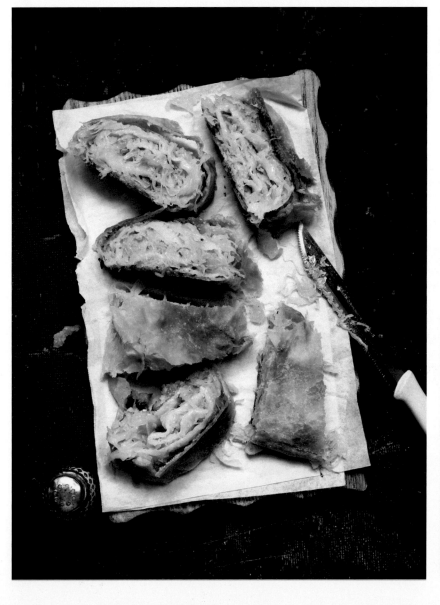

Sauerkraut strudel

Strudel is usually filled with sweet ingredients, but this savoury version is made with sauerkraut. Sauerkraut strudel tastes equally good fresh from the oven or sliced and served cold as part of an Oktoberfest party buffet.

Makes 12 pieces · Prep time: 1 hour · Resting time: 30 minutes · Baking time: 45 minutes

For the dough
250g (9oz) flour, plus extra
  for dusting
 salt
1 egg
2 tbsp vegetable oil
3 tbsp unsalted butter
2 handfuls of breadcrumbs

For the filling
sauerkraut (see p.44)

1 To make the dough, sift together the flour and salt. Add the egg, oil, and about 150ml (5fl oz) of lukewarm water. Using your hands, knead the mixture to make a moderately firm dough. Rinse a bowl with warm water, invert it over the dough, and leave to rest at room temperature for about 30 minutes.

2 Meanwhile, for the filling, prepare the sauerkraut as described on page 44 and set aside to cool. Then put it in a sieve to drain.

3 Preheat the oven to 180°C (350°F/Gas 4). Line a baking tray with baking parchment. Place the dough on the floured work surface and knead vigorously, then roll out thinly. Dust a clean tea towel with flour and place the rolled-out dough on top. Using your hands, stretch the dough as thinly as possible to form a rectangle about 40cm x 60cm (16in x 24in) in size.

4 Melt the butter and brush it onto the sheet of dough. Reserve the remaining butter. Scatter the breadcrumbs over the dough, then spread the sauerkraut evenly over the breadcrumbs. Leave a clear edge about 3cm (1in) wide so the sauerkraut doesn't escape out of the sides when you roll up the strudel. Using the tea towel, and working from the long end, roll up the dough to form a strudel. Place the strudel on the baking tray, seam-side down, and tuck the ends underneath. Brush the top with the remaining melted butter and bake the strudel in the middle of the preheated oven for about 45 minutes.

5 Remove the strudel from the oven, cut into 12 pieces, and serve. A mixed salad or pork sausages go well with this dish.

Tip: For a more substantial meal, roll up 6 grilled pork or vegetarian sausages into the strudel, along with the sauerkraut.

Potato chip spirals

with two kinds of dips

You will need a bit of patience to cut the potatoes into spirals, but it's worth the effort! The deliciously crisp spirals taste just as good at home as they do while exploring the festival grounds.

Serves 4 · Prep time: 35 minutes

For the herb dip
squeeze of fresh lemon juice
2 tbsp chopped mixed herbs
  (such as dill, parsley,
  and chives)
200g (7oz) low-fat Greek
  yogurt
salt and freshly ground
  black pepper

For the chilli dip
1 tsp smoked hot paprika
½ tsp chilli flakes
½ tsp dried thyme
200g (7oz) tomato ketchup

For the potato spirals
8–10 waxy potatoes, such
  as Charlotte
oil, for deep frying

You will also need
a spiralizer

1 To make the herb dip, stir the lemon juice and herbs into the yogurt. Season with salt and pepper.

2 To make the chilli dip, stir the paprika, chili flakes, and thyme into the ketchup. Chill both dips until ready to serve.

3 To make the potato spirals, use a spiralizer to cut the potatoes into long spirals. Pat the spirals dry with a clean tea towel.

4 In a pan, heat a generous amount of oil for deep-frying the potatoes. Working in batches, put the potato spirals into the hot oil, and as you do so, stretch them out a little. Fry the spirals for about 5 minutes until they are crisp, turning them frequently and making sure they don't stick together. Using a slotted spoon, lift the spirals out of the oil and drain on kitchen paper.

5 Sprinkle the hot potato spirals with salt or seasoning (see tip). Serve immediately, with the dips on the side.

Tip: *This quick-to-make seasoning mix gives the freshly fried potato spirals an extra twist: stir together 1 teaspoon of sugar, 1 tablespoon of paprika, ½ teaspoon of ground caraway seeds, a pinch each of cayenne pepper and salt.*

Creamy wild mushroom stew

The Bavarians call mushrooms "schwammerl" and enjoy them cooked in a creamy sauce. This mushroom stew is particularly delicious when prepared with fresh chanterelle and porcini mushrooms, which are in season during Oktoberfest.

Serves 4 · Prep time: 1 hour

1 onion
500g (1lb 2oz) mixed
  mushrooms (such as
  chanterelles, porcini,
  cremini, or white
  mushrooms)
clarified unsalted butter or
  ghee, for frying
100ml (3½fl oz) white wine
salt and freshly ground
  black pepper
400ml (14fl oz) double cream
2 tbsp chopped
  flat-leaf parsley

1   Peel the onion and dice it finely. Cut the mushrooms in half or slice them, depending on their size.

2   Heat a little clarified butter in a large frying pan. Add the onion and mushrooms and sauté over a high heat for about 5 minutes. Add the white wine to deglaze the pan and cook until the wine has completely evaporated. Only then season the mushrooms with salt and pepper. Pour in the cream and bring to the boil and simmer for about 5 minutes, or until the sauce has thickened slightly.

3   Ladle the mushroom stew into shallow bowls, sprinkle with parsley, and serve. Bread dumplings (see p.104) are the perfect accompaniment.

Tip: Creamy wild mushroom stew also makes a great sauce for pan-fried cuts of meat such as pork tenderloin medallions, rump steak, schnitzel, or strips of veal. To cook, first pan-fry the meat of your choice, remove from the pan, and keep warm. Using the same frying pan, prepare the mushroom stew as described above and serve with the meat. Classic spaetzle make a perfect side dish this (see tip, p.82).

Oktoberfest attractions: hang on tightly and don't let go!

Oktoberfest has an abundance of attractions and rides. So where should you start, and what is absolutely unmissable? Many of the fair's approximately 200 concessions have a long tradition; some have been around since the beginning of the 20th century. The traditional, nostalgic rides are particularly popular, both with locals and tourists. Often these rides have been in family hands for as many as three or four generations.

Cult rides

"Auf geht's beim Schichtl!" ("Let the Schichtl show begin!"). Many have followed this call over the years, and it has become a familiar saying in Bavaria. Since 1869, heads have literally rolled in this "original magic speciality theatre" show created by Michael August Schichtl. The short performances feature all manner of curiosities. You can watch the "beheading of a living person by means of the guillotine," or put yourself forward as a candidate for the same treatment. If that's not your thing (and in the guillotine show, it also helps to speak German), you could dress up for the Royal Bavarian Court Photographer and have your "vintage" photograph taken in period style, or be astonished by the mini-athletes in the Flohzirkus (flea circus). The action is wilder at Pitts Todeswand (Pitt's death wall), where motorcycle and go-cart daredevils have shown off their driving skills since 1928.

One fun and decidedly "cult" ride at the fair is the Teufelsrad (Devil's wheel), which has been entertaining fairgoers since 1910. The devilish part is the circular rotating platform, approximately 5m (16ft) across, on which the riders sit. The longer it rotates, the harder it is for those on the platform to resist the centrifugal

force and not slide off the platform. The riders who hold on the longest are eventually swept off by ropes and large foam balls – but the best part is the running commentary, delivered with earthy Bavarian humour by the "Rekommandeur" at the expense of the guests.

Schadenfreude – delight in the misfortune of others – is also in play on the Toboggan. This helter skelter ride has been an attraction at the fair since 1908. The wooden slide is in itself quite harmless, but getting to the top requires a ride on a mean and very fast-moving conveyor belt. If you've had a few beers, it can definitely put a dent in your performance! While women usually have the support of helpful gentlemen, men tend to be left to their own devices – and often succeed admirably in making fools of themselves. They flail around helplessly trying to hold on to the railing that doesn't actually move with the conveyor belt, leading them to travel to the top feet- or bottom-first. Incidentally, the name "Toboggan" comes from the language of the native Algonquin in Canada and means "snow sled."

Perhaps it's best to avoid disgrace and climb aboard the Krinoline instead. Moving gently up and down as it revolves to the comfortable tempo of a live brass band, this old-fashioned carousel has been an attraction for almost a century. Its name is a reference to the bouncing hooped skirts worn by women in the second half of the 19th century. In the first years after its introduction to the fair in 1924, the Munich Krinoline was operated solely by muscle power, but in 1937 it was electrified. The brass band was hired shortly afterwards by Michael Großmann, the concession owner at the time. Since then, the ride has been accompanied by Bavarian mood music.

Hi-tech tests of courage

For high-end thrill seekers with cast-iron stomachs, the fair offers a huge adrenaline rush in the shape of an enormous number of modern rides. "Higher, further, faster", they shout as they clamber aboard Cyber Space, Top Spin, High Energy, or Frisbee. These popular, dizzying thrill rides take you up, down, to the right, to the left, and upside down, and are really only recommended for those with the hardiest constitution.

It's also possible "just" to go round and round – albeit fast. Some of these more nostalgic rides take you "Rund um the Tegernsee" (around Lake Tegernsee), or on the Zugspitzbahn (Zugspitze train), around a winter landscape complete with snowman. You can't be afraid of heights if you decide to ride up the Skyfall-Turm (Skyfall tower) or the Power Tower II to platforms 80m (265ft) high, only to plunge down to earth at a terrifying speed. For a similar effect on your stomach, try one of the many other roller coasters. Among them is the Olympia-Looping, supposedly the largest travelling roller coaster in the world. It incorporates five vertical loops and reaches a speed of more than 100kph (60mph). It has had a permanent slot on the fairgrounds since 1989. Another institution is

the popular Alpinabahn (Alpine train), which, instead of turning riders upside down, hurtles them downhill at a breathtaking speed.

High up in the air

Rather than plummeting earthward, some might prefer gliding through the air instead. So it's off to a ride on the good old Kettenkarussell – the swing ride! The Kalb family set up their first swing ride on the Theresienwiese in 1919. It was replaced in 2004 by the more modern wave swinger, Circus Welt. The soft clinking of the steel chains when the seats bump into one another, the wind in your hair, and the candied almonds you can nibble on during a flight make this a favourite for many visitors to the fairgrounds – that and all the other classics, of course, such as the bumper cars and the swing boat. Last, but not least, there's the Ferris wheel, an absolute must for romantics. When you are as high as 50m (165ft) up in the air, the gondolas, decorated with hearts and blue-and-white checks, offer a sensational view over the Theresienwiese, especially after dark, when it is illuminated by millions of lights. It offers a great view over Munich, and is good family fun, too.

There are also many attractions for the youngest fans of the fair, from the blue-and-white Münchner Rutsch'n with its wavy slides and the various children's carousels, to the Wilde Maus (wild mouse) – which is actually enjoyed by many adults, too. For horror fans of all ages, the Geisterbahn (ghost train), a haunted house ride, is the place to go: the bravest choose one featuring "live" ghosts (played by actors). The Irrgarten, or fun house, sometimes turns into a test even for adult visitors. You can also try your luck at one of the many shooting stands and other carnival games. You'll be popular with the little ones if you win a stuffed toy at one of these.

The "Old fair"

Since 2010, the Oktoberfest has been enriched by another popular attraction, perhaps *the* most popular: the "Oide Wiesn," or old fair. This amusement park, with its rides and beer tents that take you back to the olden days of the Oktoberfest, was set up in the south section of the Theresienwiese in 2010 to mark the 200th anniversary of the festival. It was so well received that it was made a permanent part of the Oktoberfest. Every four years it has to make way for the Bavarian Agricultural Fair, which takes place on the same spot. The "Old Fair" is different: Here things are slower and gentler, traditionally Bavarian, and with a great atmosphere. In the two popular tents, Tradition and Herzkasperl, beer is served in ceramic mugs, or steins,

as it was in the past. And people don't dance on the benches, but on the dedicated dance floor or in front of the stage. Bands come from all over Bavaria to perform here. The Herzkasperl tent offers a platform for younger artists, some of whom are from the regional music scene, like Hasemanns Töchter or G. Rag & die Landlergschwister. In the Tradition tent, great brass bands, folk dance groups, and whip-crackers provide the atmosphere. Another attraction is the "Humoristische Velodrom"; the fun bike races held here require equal amounts of speed and dexterity. In front of the tent, old-fashioned rides, ring tossing, and similar pleasures vie for the attention of the public.

Here you will also find the original Kalb swing ride dating back to 1919, and a ride on the vintage Calypso, with its colourful, decorated gondolas, will make you feel like you are back in the 1960s. With its marionette theatre, pony run, swing boat, old-fashioned carousel, and varied entertainment, the historic fair has a great deal to offer, especially for children and families. For a modest entrance fee of €3 (£2) you can stay in the grounds of the traditional fair all day long, from 10am to 10pm. The rides themselves usually cost €1 (70p), so all in all, this is affordable fun. Concessions stop serving alcohol at around 9:30pm, an hour earlier than on the main fairgrounds. This might seem a bit early, but it has one definite advantage: you can go to bed earlier and be fit enough the next day to return for more celebrating.

Grünkern (spelt) patties
with paprika

Year after year, you will find more vegetarian and vegan food at Oktoberfest, such as these patties made with grünkern, or unripe spelt. It has always been a popular ingredient in vegetarian dishes in Bavarian cuisine.

oil, for frying
250g (9oz) medium whole
  grünkern groats (unripe
  crushed spelt grains with
  the husks removed)
500ml (16fl oz) vegetable
  stock
1 onion
1 red pepper
3 sprigs of thyme
salt and freshly ground
  black pepper
2 large eggs
100g (3½oz) grated
  Emmental cheese
2–3 tbsp breadcrumbs
1 tbsp paprika

Serves 4 · Prep time: 50 minutes

1 Heat 1 tablespoon of oil in a pan and sauté the grünkern until lightly browned. Pour in the vegetable stock and simmer the groats over a low heat, stirring constantly, for about 5 minutes. Remove the pan from the heat and leave the grünkern to swell for about 20 minutes, then set aside to cool.

2 Meanwhile, peel the onion and remove the stem and seeds from the red pepper. Finely dice the onion and pepper. In a frying pan, heat 1 tablespoon of oil, add the onion, and sauté for a few minutes. Then add the diced pepper and thyme. Season with salt and pepper and remove the thyme sprigs.

3 In a large bowl, combine the cooked grünkern, pepper and onion mixture, eggs, cheese, and breadcrumbs, until you have a mixture that is easy to shape. Season with salt, pepper, and paprika, then moisten your hands and make 8 patties from the spelt mixture.

4 Heat a little oil in a large frying pan, add the spelt patties, and fry them on each side for about 10 minutes. Remove from the frying pan and serve with carrot and cabbage salad (see p.100). If you like, serve a dip alongside (see p.86).

Creamy Savoy cabbage
with fried eggs

In Bavaria, fried eggs are often called "ox eyes". The eggs turn the creamy cabbage into a main dish; without them, it also makes a great side for many meat dishes.

Serves 4 · Prep time: 45 minutes

1 small head of Savoy cabbage
  (about 600g/1lb 5oz)
salt and freshly ground
  black pepper
2 carrots
1 onion
unsalted butter for frying
1 tbsp plain flour
400ml (14fl oz)
  vegetable stock
200ml (7fl oz) double cream
grated nutmeg
1 tsp caraway seeds
4–8 eggs
paprika, to serve

1   Cut the cabbage into square pieces about 2 x 2cm (¾ x ¾in) and slice the carrots. In a large pan, bring salted water to the boil. Blanch the cabbage pieces in the boiling water until al dente. Drain the cabbage in a sieve, plunge into ice water, and drain again. Repeat with the carrot slices.

2   Peel the onion and dice it finely. Melt 1 tablespoon of butter in a pan, add the onion, and sauté for a few minutes. Dust the onion with flour and pour in the vegetable broth. Stirring constantly, simmer the sauce for about 10 minutes. Stir in the cream.

3   Add the Savoy cabbage and carrots to the sauce. Season the vegetables with salt, pepper, nutmeg, and caraway seeds, and simmer for about 5 minutes.

4   Heat a little butter in a large frying pan (you may have to do this in two portions, or two frying pans). Break the eggs gently into the pans and fry them over a low heat for about 5 minutes until the whites have set.

5   Portion out the creamy cabbage onto plates, top each with a fried egg or two, and sprinkle with paprika, to taste. Serve with salt and pepper, for the eggs, and parslied potatoes (see p.103).

Tip: Creamy Savoy cabbage tastes good as a side for beef roulades (see p.61), for example, or venison stew (see p.65), or stuffed breast of veal (see p.54).

Red cabbage

Serves 4 · Prep time: 25 minutes · Cooking time: 45 minutes

1 small head of red cabbage,
   about 800g (1¾lb)
1 onion
2 apples
2 tbsp vegetable oil
200ml (7fl oz) red wine
500ml (16fl oz)
   vegetable stock
salt
½ tsp black peppercorns
1 clove
1 bay leaf
1 tbsp cornstarch
2 tbsp cooked cranberries,
   lingonberries, or fresh red
   currants

1 Slice the cabbage into very thin strips. Peel the onion and slice into rings. Quarter and core the apples, and cut the quarters into thin slices.

2 Heat the oil in a large pan. Add the onion and apples, and sauté for a few minutes. Add the cabbage and sauté it briefly. Pour in the red wine to deglaze the pan and boil until it has completely evaporated. Pour in the vegetable stock, season with salt, peppercorns, clove, and bay leaf, and simmer over a low heat for about 45 minutes, stirring occasionally.

3 Stir 2 tablespoons of cold water into the cornstarch. Stir the cornstarch mixture into the cabbage and boil for about 5 minutes.

4 Just before serving, fold the cooked cranberries, lingonberries, or fresh red currants into the cabbage. Red cabbage goes well with dishes such as crispy duck (see p.70), venison stew (see p.65), or sauerbraten (see p.58).

Bavarian cabbage

Serves 4 · Prep time: 20 minutes · Cooking time: 45 minutes

1 small head of white cabbage
   (about 800g/1¾lb)
1 onion
2 tbsp vegetable oil
1 tsp sugar
1 tsp caraway seeds
500ml (16fl oz) vegetable
   stock
salt
1 tbsp white wine vinegar

1 Cut the cabbage into square pieces of about 2 x 2cm (¾ x ¾in). Peel the onion and slice into rings.

2 Heat the oil in a large pan, add the onion, and sauté for a few minutes. Sprinkle the sugar over the onions and fry them until golden brown and lightly caramelized. Add the cabbage and caraway seeds and fry briefly. Then pour in the vegetable stock and simmer the cabbage over a low heat for about 45 minutes, stirring ocasionally. Season with salt.

3 Just before serving, stir in the white wine vinegar. Bavarian cabbage is a great alternative to sauerkraut for dishes such as roast suckling pig (see p.47), roast ham hocks (see tip, p.74), or boiled ham hocks (see p.44).

Bavarian cabbage slaw

Serves 4 · Prep time: 20 minutes

1 small head of white cabbage
  (about 800g/1¾lb)
salt and freshly ground
  black pepper
4 tbsp white wine vinegar
4 tbsp vegetable oil
1 tsp caraway seeds

1 Cut the cabbage into very thin strips and put into a bowl. Salt generously. Using your hands, vigorously knead the cabbage for about 5 minutes until it has softened and become glassy in appearance.

2 Add the vinegar and oil to the cabbage, and toss. Season the salad with pepper and caraway seeds, and leave it to marinate for about 15 minutes. The slaw goes very well with dishes such as roast ham hocks (see tip p.74), roast suckling pig (see p.47), or stuffed breast of veal (see p.54).

Tip: *For some extra crunch, cut 150g (5½oz) of well-marbled smoked bacon or smoked tofu into small cubes. Heat 1 tablespoon of oil in a frying pan, add the bacon or tofu, and fry until crisp. Add the bacon or tofu to the slaw, toss, and marinate as described above, but use only 3 tablespoons of vegetable oil for the marinade.*

Carrot and cabbage slaw

Serves 4 · Prep time: 20 minutes

½ head of white cabbage
  (about 400g/14oz)
salt and freshly ground
  black pepper
4 carrots
4 tbsp apple vinegar
4 tbsp vegetable oil
1 tsp sugar
2 tbsp chopped
  flat-leaf parsley

1 Cut the cabbage into very thin strips and put into a bowl. Salt generously. Using your hands, vigorously knead the cabbage for about 5 minutes until the cabbage has softened and become glassy in appearance.

2 Grate the carrots and add them to the cabbage. Stir in the vinegar and oil, and toss well. Season with pepper to taste, add the sugar, toss well, and leave to marinate for about 15 minutes.

3 Just before serving, sprinkle parsley over the slaw. Carrot and cabbage slaw is good with dishes such as pork schnitzel cordon bleu (see p.43) or spelt patties (see p.94).

Tip: *Do you like your salad a little fruity? Then grate 1 apple and add it to the cabbage along with the carrots.*

Parslied potatoes

Serves 4 · Prep time: 30 minutes

800g (1¾lb) waxy potatoes,
  such as Charlotte
salt
2 tbsp unsalted butter
2 tbsp chopped
  flat-leaf parsley

1 Peel and wash the potatoes. Depending on their size, cut them into halves or quarters. Boil the potatoes in salted water for about 20 minutes, or until cooked, then drain.

2 Melt the butter in a large frying pan and heat until it foams. Add the potatoes and parsley, and shake the frying pan back and forth until the potatoes are coated on all sides with the parsley butter. Parslied potatoes go very well with dishes such as boiled beef (see p.57), boiled ham hocks (see p.44), or pan-fried char (see p.77).

Classic mashed potatoes

Serves 4 · Prep time: 30 minutes

1kg (2.2lb) floury potatoes,
  such as Maris Piper
salt
250ml (9fl oz) whole milk
2 tbsp unsalted butter
pinch of grated nutmeg

1 Peel and wash the potatoes. Depending on their size, cut them into halves or quarters. Boil in salted water for about 20 minutes, or until cooked. Drain the potatoes and mash well with a potato masher.

2 Boil the milk. Stir the butter into the potatoes. Then pour over the hot milk and stir. Finally, season the mash with freshly grated nutmeg. Classic mashed potatoes go well with sauce-rich dishes such as beef roulades (see p.61), sauerbraten (see p.58), boiled ham hocks on a bed of sauerkraut (see p.44), or just on their own, topped with fried onions.

Dumpling essentials

Potato dumplings

Serves 4 · Prep time: 1 hour

1.5kg (3.3lb) floury potatoes,
  such as Maris Piper
salt
½ roll of day-old bread
1 tbsp unsalted butter

1 Peel and wash half the potatoes. Depending on their size, halve or quarter them. Boil in salted water for 20 minutes, or until cooked, and drain. Return them to the pot for about 5 minutes to let the steam evaporate, then put them through a potato ricer, or mash thoroughly with a potato masher.

2 Peel, wash, and finely grate the remaining potatoes. Put the grated potato on a clean tea towel and twist the ends of the towel together. Working over a bowl, squeeze the liquid from the potatoes, then set the bowl of liquid aside for five minutes until the starch separates. Carefully pour away the liquid at the top, leaving the potato starch behind.

3 Combine the boiled and raw potatoes and the potato starch from the bowl. Season the mixture with salt to taste.

4 Cut the bread roll into small cubes. Melt the butter in a frying pan, add the bread, and fry until golden brown. Remove the cubes from the pan.

5 Bring salted water to the boil in a large pan. Shape peach-size dumplings from the mixture, press a few bread cubes into the centre of each, reshape, drop into the boiling water, and simmer over a low heat for 20 minutes or until cooked. Lift out of the water with a slotted spoon and serve. Potato dumplings make an excellent side dish for all sauce-rich meat dishes.

Bread dumplings

Makes 4 portions · Prep time: 45 minutes

8 rolls of day-old bread
250ml (9fl oz) whole milk
1 onion
1 tbsp unsalted butter
2 large eggs
2 tbsp chopped
  flat-leaf parsley
salt and freshly ground
  black pepper
pinch of grated nutmeg

1 Finely slice the bread rolls and put them in a bowl. Boil the milk, pour it over the bread, mix thoroughly, and leave to soak for about 15 minutes.

2 Peel the onion and dice it finely. Melt the butter in a frying pan, add the onion, and sauté. Add the fried onion, eggs, and parsley to the bread-and-milk mixture. Combine thoroughly and season with salt, pepper, and nutmeg.

3 Bring salted water to the boil in a large pan. Shape peach-sized dumplings from the bread mixture. Drop the dumplings in the boiling water and simmer over a low heat for about 20 minutes until they are cooked. Lift out of the water with a slotted spoon and serve with roast suckling pig (see p.47), sauerbraten (see p.58), or creamy wild mushroom stew (see p.89), for example.

Vegetable-stuffed ravioli
with fried onions

These ravioli have a delectable vegetable filling. Rolling out the dough and filling the pasta requires some preparation time, but you'll be rewarded with an incomparable treat!

Serves 4 · Prep time: 1 hour

For the pasta
300g (10½oz) plain flour, plus extra for dusting
100g (3½oz) semolina
salt and freshly ground black pepper
5 eggs
1 tbsp vegetable oil

For the filling
2 rolls of day-old bread
2 carrots, about 125g (4½oz) each
¼ celeriac, about 125g (4½oz)
1 leek, about 180g (6oz)
1 tbsp unsalted butter
2 tbsp chopped flat-leaf parsley
2 large eggs
handful of breadcrumbs
pinch of grated nutmeg

To serve
2 onions
3 tbsp unsalted butter
2 tbsp chopped flat-leaf parsley

You will also need
a pasta maker

1 To make the pasta, combine the flour, semolina, and salt in a bowl. Add 4 eggs and the oil, and knead for about 5 minutes to make a moderately firm dough. Cover in cling film and rest in the fridge for about 30 minutes.

2 To make the filling, put the bread rolls in a bowl of water and soak for about 30 minutes. Meanwhile, finely dice the carrots, celeriac, and leek. Melt the butter in a large frying pan, add the diced vegetables, and sauté for about 10 minutes. Put the vegetables in a bowl and set aside to cool.

3 Squeeze the soaked bread to remove the excess water, and purée. Combine the bread, diced vegetables, parsley, eggs, and breadcrumbs. Season the mixture with salt, pepper, and nutmeg and set aside until needed.

4 Cut the dough in half. Use a pasta maker to make 2 very thin sheets of pasta about 1mm (1⁄16in) thick. Alternatively, roll out the dough on the floured work surface to make very thin sheets. Place one sheet on the work surface. Drop heaped tablespoonfuls of the vegetable mixture all over the sheet, leaving a large gap between spoonfuls. Whisk the remaining egg and brush it onto the pasta in the gaps between fillings. Place the second sheet of dough on top and press down gently. Cut out squares about 6 x 6cm (¼ x ¼in) in size and press the edges together. Place the ravioli side by side on a floured baking tray.

5 Bring a large pan of salted water to the boil. Add the ravioli and simmer over a low heat for about 5 minutes, until they are cooked.

6 In the meantime, peel the onions and dice them finely. Melt 1 tablespoon of the butter in a frying pan, add the diced onions, and sauté until golden brown. Melt the remaining butter in one large, or two small, frying pans. Using a slotted spoon, remove the ravioli from the water and drain, then fry them in the hot butter. Sprinkle the pan-fried onions and parsley over the ravioli and serve. A green salad goes well with this dish.

Tip: If you don't have much patience for dicing vegetables, here's a little shortcut: simply grate the carrots and celeriac, and slice the leek into very thin rings.

From flirting to toasting: surviving Oktoberfest

At this kind of festival, it is very tempting to get carried away by celebrating spontaneously and with a carefree attitude, and not giving etiquette too much of a thought. However, this is a bit shortsighted: enjoyment, too, is an art that can be mastered. Bear in mind a few simple rules and tricks and you will get the most out of your evening and be pleasant company for friends, acquaintances, or work colleagues.

Go easy on the beer

Oktoberfest beer is strong and will make you drunk far more quickly than regular beer. Depending on your age, gender, and constitution, even one or two mass may be enough to get you quite inebriated; a third or more could be a step too far.

The most important beer tent rule is simple: know your limits – don't drink more than you can handle. A mass doesn't have to be emptied completely: leave the dregs (the Bavarians call this the "noagerl") and order a fresh one. After all, you don't want to spend an evening at the fair nursing stale beer, and clinking glasses is more fun with a fresh mass. You don't necessarily have to overindulge though – in practically all the tents, the waiters will also serve "radler" or shandy, as well as alcohol-free beer.

Whether you are in the company of colleagues or friends, here's another important drinking rule to remember: take it slow. Lining your stomach – perhaps with a decent "brotzeit" (see p.12) – is essential. When you order your first beer, it's a good idea to order something to eat at the same time. In any case, a table reservation comes not only with coupons for two litres of beer, each guest also receives a "chicken coupon" – a food coupon worth at

least €10 (£7). Here's another tip: don't start with a beer, but make the first mass a shandy. After finishing your food, you can still order beer.

Yet another important Oktoberfest rule is not to be too stingy with your tips. The waiters work very hard, often carrying 10 or 12 full litre-mugs of beer through the swaying crowds, and balancing trays laden with 18 chickens from one end of the tent to the other. Be generous – the servers really do appreciate it.

Friendly toasting

By the way, drinking within reason doesn't mean clinging to your first mug of beer for hours to make it last, or not clinking glasses with the people around you. When the refrain "Prosit der Gemütlichkeit" (which translates as "here's to coziness") sounds – which seems to happen about every seven minutes! – you should go along with it: it's part of the experience, and you can always take small sips if you prefer. When you're clinking glasses, look the other person in the eye and hold your beer mug by the handle – don't use your thumb and palm as you do when drinking, or your fingers may get squashed.

A bad habit that's becoming more common is drinking before the fair, either to get into the spirit of things more quickly, or because bottled beer is cheap compared with a mass at the fair. As ever, the "what" and "how much" matters: a glass of sparkling wine beforehand certainly won't hurt, but a few shots of hard liquor, such as schnapps or vodka, can mean that the fun is all over by the second mass of beer.

Flirting at Oktoberfest

So what's the word on flirting at the fair? Well, almost nowhere else is it easier to find a partner. After one or two mass, inhibitions fall, and any language barriers seem to disappear. The locals, too, have just as much fun as the tourists getting to know people from other countries. In fact, many a marriage has its beginnings at Oktoberfest! If you are visiting the fair with your partner, it's a good idea to clearly show that you are in a relationship to avoid any awkward scenes. For everyone else, though, it's high flirt-alert! Women dressed in dirndls should definitely make use of the bows of their aprons to send clear signals (see p.23). A bow tied on the right means "I am already spoken for," but a bow tied on the left means "I'm single – and may be happy to accept a compliment or two from you."

It's better not to:

· Bid for a table at an online auction, as it isn't secure. Book directly with the tent landlords instead (see p.138)

· Hire your Bavarian costume from a carnival-costume rental company, if you want it to be authentic

· Be a cheapskate when tipping

· Be disrespectful when addressing the waiters and waitresses

· Smoke in a beer tent – it's strictly forbidden

· Hold the beer mug with two hands when drinking from it – the beer will warm up very quickly

· Climb onto the table to dance instead of onto the bench

· Try to flirt with women who have their dirndl bow tied on the right-hand side

· Argue with the security guards

· Fall asleep at the table

· Get into a fight – if you feel uncomfortable with a situation, ask a security guard for help

· Steal a beer mug

· Go to the toilet where it's not allowed

· Sleep it off outdoors near Theresienhöhe

Bavarian potato salad

Potato salad makes a good side for many Bavarian dishes and is also delicious on its own. Depending on seasonal availability, try adding endives, celeriac, or even chanterelle mushrooms.

Serves 4 · Prep time: 25 minutes · Marinating time: 20 minutes

750g (1¾lb) waxy potatoes,
  such as Charlotte
salt and freshly ground
  black pepper
1 onion
4 tbsp vegetable oil
3 tbsp white wine vinegar
250ml (9fl oz) vegetable stock
1 tbsp medium-hot mustard
2 tbsp chopped chives

1 Boil the potatoes, unpeeled, in salted water for about 20 minutes, or until cooked. Drain, allow the steam to evaporate, and peel. Set aside the potatoes to cool a little, then cut them into slices and put them in a bowl.

2 Peel the onion and dice it finely. Heat the oil in a frying pan and sauté the onion for a few minutes. Add the vinegar and vegetable broth, stir in the mustard, and bring to the boil. Pour the hot marinade over the sliced potatoes and toss gently. Season the potato salad with salt and pepper and leave to marinate for about 20 minutes.

3 Sprinkle chives over the potato salad. Serve with dishes such as pork schnitzel cordon bleu (see p.43), beer battered fish (see p.78), or Oktoberfest chicken (see p.74).

Variations: Prepare the potato salad as described above, but instead of sprinkling it with chives, stir in one of the following:

Potato and endive salad
Slice ¼ of a head of endive into strips and stir into the potato salad.

Potato and celeriac salad
Peel ½ of a celeriac and cut it into bite-sized pieces. Blanch the celeriac in boiling salted water and stir into the sliced potatoes. Leave to marinate for 20 minutes.

Potato salad with chanterelles and bacon
Heat 1 tbsp vegetable oil in a frying pan. Add 150g (5½oz) of diced smoked bacon and sauté until crisp. Add 200g (7oz) of chanterelle mushrooms and sauté for a few minutes. Season with salt and pepper, and stir into the potato salad.

Pretzel cheese sticks,
snails, and chestnuts

Mini pretzel cheese pastries – formed into different shapes – are very easy to make and taste great as a snack. Of course, you can also twist the dough into traditional pretzels if you like (see variation).

Makes 8 pieces · Prep time: 1 hour · Rising time: 1 hour 30 minutes · Baking time: 15 minutes

For the dough
500g (1lb 2oz) plain flour, plus extra for dusting
20g (¾oz) fresh yeast or 1 tsp active dry yeast
pinch of sugar
2 tbsp vegetable oil
salt
1 tbsp baking soda

For sprinkling
150g (5½oz) grated Emmental cheese
coarse sea salt
sesame seeds
poppy seeds
sunflower seeds

1 Sift the flour into a large mixing bowl and make a well in the centre. Crumble the fresh yeast or active dry yeast into the well and add a pinch of sugar and a little lukewarm water. Stir with a fork, incorporating some flour from the sides of the well, to make a starter. Cover the bowl with a clean tea towel and leave to rise in a warm place for about 15 minutes.

2 Add the oil, salt, and about 200ml (7fl oz) of lukewarm water to the bowl and stir to combine. Then, using your hands, knead the dough on a floured work surface until smooth and elastic. Put in an oiled bowl, cover with a clean tea towel, and leave to rise in a warm place for about 1 hour.

3 Knead the dough once more and divide it into 8 pieces. To make cheese pretzel sticks, form thick ropes about 15cm (6in) long and 5cm (2in) thick. To make pretzel snails, form thick ropes about 20cm (8in) long and 3cm (1in) thick and curl them up to make snail shapes. For chestnuts, roll the dough into balls.

4 Preheat the oven to 200°C (400°F/Gas 6). Line a baking tray with baking parchment and dust with flour. Arrange the pretzel cheese sticks, snails, and chestnuts on the baking tray. Cover the tray and leave to rise for 15 minutes.

5 Put 250ml (9fl oz) of water and the baking soda in a pan and bring to the boil. Brush the cheese sticks, snails, and chestnuts generously with the solution.

6 Make a lenthways cut in the cheese sticks lengthwise, open out a little, and sprinkle grated cheese into the cut. Slice a cross into the tops of the chestnuts. Sprinkle the chestnuts and the snails with salt, sesame, poppy, or sunflower seeds. Bake in the middle of the oven for about 15 minutes. These mini pretzels go well with beer, a Brotzeit platter (see p.12), or Oktoberfest chicken (see p.74).

Variation: For pretzels, roll the dough portions into ropes about 40cm (16in) long and 3cm (1in) thick. Shape into pretzels, brush with the soda solution, and bake as above. The solution is harmless, but avoid any contact with foil so you don't get an unwanted chemical reaction.

Sweet treats and baked goods

Strauben

Makes 10 pieces · Prep time: 50 minutes

50g (1¾oz) unsalted butter
1 tbsp caster sugar
pinch of salt
150g (5½oz) flour
4 eggs
oil, for deep frying
250g (9oz) icing sugar
3 tbsp rum

You will also need
a piping bag with a star nozzle

1 Put 250ml (9fl oz) of water, the butter, sugar, and the salt in a pan and bring to the boil. Add all the flour and stir immediately with a wooden spoon until smooth. Continue to stir vigorously on the hob until the dough forms a ball and a white film appears on the bottom of the pan. Remove from the hob and leave the dough to cool a little.

2 Cut out 10 squares of baking parchment, about 10cm x 10cm (4in x 4in). Stir the eggs into the dough one at a time. Fill the piping bag with the dough and pipe circles about 8cm (3in) in diameter onto each square of paper.

3 In a shallow pan, heat enough oil to deep-fry the dough. One after the other, slide the strauben into the hot oil, paper side up, and fry for about 5 minutes, or until golden brown. Turn them over and fry on the other side for about 2 minutes, until cooked. Pull away any loose pieces of paper. Using a slotted spoon, lift the strauben out of the oil and drain on kitchen paper.

4 Stir together the icing sugar and rum until smooth and use the mixture to glaze the strauben.

Tip: This almost-forgotten, deep-fried treat made from choux pastry is traditionally made in autumn and winter. You can use lemon juice instead of rum for the glaze, or dust the strauben with icing sugar.

Quark doughnut balls

Makes 20 pieces · Prep time: 35 minutes

250g (9oz) plain flour
1 tsp baking powder
3 eggs
120g (4½oz) caster sugar
250g (9oz) full-fat quark
  (alternatively, use a thick
  and creamy full-fat yogurt)
zest of ½ lemon
whole milk (as needed)
oil, for deep frying
1 tsp ground cinnamon

1 Mix together the flour and baking powder. Beat the eggs with 60g (2¼oz) of the sugar until foamy. Stir in the flour mixture, quark, and lemon zest. If the dough is too firm, stir in a little milk.

2 In a shallow pan, heat up enough oil to deep-fry the dough. Using two tablespoons, shape small balls from the dough and drop them into the hot oil. Fry for about 5 minutes until golden brown on all sides. Using a slotted spoon, lift the balls out of the oil and drain on kitchen paper.

3 Stir together the remaining sugar and the cinnamon. Roll the hot quark balls in the mixture until they are completely covered.

Dessert dumplings

with a sweet honey crust

You won't be able to resist the mouth-watering, sweet aroma of these divine dumplings as it wafts through the air at the fairground or in your home. They are best served with home-made vanilla sauce.

Serves 12 · Prep time: 45 minutes · Rising time: 1 hour 15 minutes ·
Baking time: 50 minutes

500g (1lb 2oz) plain flour, plus
    extra for dusting
20g (¾oz) fresh yeast or 1 tsp
    active dry yeast
100g (3½oz) caster sugar
250ml (9fl oz) lukewarm whole
    milk, plus extra for baking
100g (3½oz) unsalted butter,
    plus extra for greasing
2 large eggs
zest of 1 lemon
3 tbsp honey

To serve
500ml (16fl oz) vanilla sauce
    (from a packet mix or home-
    made, see tip)

1 Sift the flour into a large mixing bowl and make a well in the centre. Crumble the yeast into the well and add a pinch of the sugar and a little of the lukewarm milk. Stir with a fork, incorporating some flour from the sides of the well, to make a yeast starter. Cover the bowl with a clean tea towel and leave to rise in a warm place for 15 minutes or so.

2 Melt the butter. Add half of the butter, the remaining milk, 50g (1¾oz) of the sugar, the eggs, and the lemon zest to the starter, and stir until the dough comes together. Using your hands, knead the dough on a floured work surface until smooth and elastic. Put into an oiled bowl, cover with a clean tea towel, and leave to rise in a warm place for about 1 hour.

3 Generously butter the sides of an ovenproof casserole dish. Put the remaining melted butter and sugar in a small pan and stir over a low heat until caramelized and light brown in colour. Remove from the stove and stir in the honey. Pour the caramel mixture into the casserole dish and set aside to cool.

4 Preheat the oven to 180°C (350°F/Gas 4). Knead the dough briefly, then divide into 12 pieces and shape each piece into a slightly flattened dumpling. Arrange the dumplings side by side on top of the caramel. Pour about 125ml (4fl oz) of milk into the dish, cover it tightly with a lid or foil, and bake the dumplings in the middle of the oven for about 50 minutes. Remove the dumplings from the casserole dish one at a time and turn each over so the honey crust is on top. Serve with vanilla sauce (see tip).

Tip: *To make vanilla sauce, bring 500ml (16fl oz) of milk to the boil in a pan. Slit open a vanilla pod, scrape out the seeds, and add to the milk. Whisk together 6 egg yolks and 2 tablespoons of sugar in a bowl, then stir the hot milk slowly into the egg mixture. Pour back into the pan and, stirring constantly with a wooden spoon, heat to about 70°C (160°F). The sauce is ready when it coats the back of the wooden spoon and rose-shaped waves form when you blow on it. Immediately take it off the hob, pour through a fine mesh sieve, and serve.*

Millirahmstrudel

with a classic filling

This juicy strudel originated in Vienna, but today it is a well-established Oktoberfest classic. It is delicious eaten warm or cold, and best served with a nice cup of coffee.

Serves 12 · Prep time: 45 minutes · Resting time: 30 minutes · Baking time: 45 minutes

For the dough
1 recipe strudel dough
   (see p.85)
3 tbsp unsalted butter, plus
   more for the baking dish
flour for dusting
1–2 handfuls of breadcrumbs

For the filling
3 eggs
100g (3½oz) softened
   unsalted butter
100g (3½oz) caster sugar
500g (1lb 2oz) quark
   (alternatively, use a thick
   and creamy, plain,
   low-fat yogurt)
300g (10½oz) soured cream
zest of 1 lemon
75g (2½oz) raisins

For the glaze
2 eggs
200ml (7fl oz) milk
1 sachet vanilla sugar or
   1 tsp pure vanilla extract

1   Prepare the strudel dough and set aside to rest for 30 minutes.

2   Meanwhile, make the filling. Separate the eggs and beat the egg whites in a bowl until they form stiff peaks. In a separate bowl, beat the butter and sugar together until fluffy, then beat in the egg yolks one at a time. Stir in the quark, soured cream, lemon zest, and raisins. Fold in the beaten egg whites.

3   Preheat the oven to 180°C (350°F/Gas 4). Generously butter an ovenproof dish. Knead the dough again on a floured work surface and roll it out. Dust a clean tea towel with flour, place the sheet of dough on top, and stretch as thinly as possible with your hands to make a rectangle about 40cm x 60cm (16in x 24in).

4   In a small pan, melt the butter over a low heat and brush it on the sheet of dough, then sprinkle the dough with breadcrumbs. Spread the filling evenly over the dough, leaving a clear edge about 3cm (1in) wide. With the aid of the tea towel, and working from the long end, roll up the dough to form a strudel. Place the strudel on the baking dish, seam-side down, and tuck the ends underneath.

5   To make the glaze, whisk the eggs with the milk, vanilla sugar or vanilla extract, and pour the mixture over the strudel. Bake the strudel in the middle of the oven for about 45 minutes. Remove from the oven and cut into 12 pieces. Enjoy warm straight from the oven, or serve cold.

French toast

with plum butter and cinnamon sugar

Originally, this Bavarian version of French toast, called "bavesen", was served on farms at Candlemas (2nd of February). On this day, the farm servants received their yearly pay, and the farmers' wives made bavesen to thank them for all their hard work.

Serves 4 · Prep time: 25 minutes

8 slices of day-old
 white bread
4 tbsp plum butter or
 plum jam
2 large eggs
1 tbsp plain flour
250ml (9fl oz) whole milk
2 tbsp caster sugar
½ tsp ground cinnamon
clarified unsalted butter or
 ghee, for frying

1 Lay out 4 slices of bread on a board and spread each slice with 1 tablespoon of plum butter. Top with another slice of bread and press together lightly.

2 Whisk together the eggs and flour in a shallow bowl. Pour the milk into a second shallow bowl. Mix together the sugar and cinnamon on a plate.

3 Heat a generous amount of clarified butter in a large frying pan. Dip both sides of each sandwich into the milk until well soaked. Then dip both sides into the egg mixture and transfer immediately to the hot butter in the pan. Fry for about 5 minutes on each side until golden brown. Lift out of the pan and drain on kitchen paper, then dredge the hot French toast in the cinnamon sugar mix, and serve immediately.

Tip: French toast also tastes delicious when prepared with braided buns or wholewheat bread instead of white bread. For a different filling, try other fruit jams, plum compote (see p.124), or slices of fresh banana.

Fluffy kaiserschmarrn
with plum compote

Despite feeling full, people will always find enough room for a few bites of freshly cooked "kaiserschmarrn", a kind of shredded pancake with enticing aromas. You can even serve it as a main course!

Serves 4 as a main course or 6–8 as a dessert · Prep time: 1 hour

For the plum compote
1kg (2.2lb) plums
4 tbsp caster sugar
1 cinnamon stick
2 cloves

For the kaiserschmarrn
200g (7oz) plain flour
1 tbsp caster sugar
pinch of salt
200ml (7fl oz) whole milk
4 eggs
clarified unsalted butter or
   ghee, for frying
handful of raisins, soaked in
   rum for at least 1 hour
handful of slivered almonds
icing sugar, to serve

1 To make the plum compote, halve the plums and remove the stones. Put the sugar and 3 tablespoons of water in a pan and heat, without stirring, until caramelized. Add the plums, cinnamon stick, and cloves, and bring to the boil.

2 Reduce the heat and simmer the plums for about 5 minutes, stirring occasionally, until the juice has thickened but the plums have not yet completely disintegrated. Remove the compote from the hob and set aside to cool.

3 To make the kaiserschmarrn, combine the flour, sugar, and salt in a bowl. Add the milk and whisk to make a thick batter.

4 Separate the eggs and whip the egg whites in a big bowl until they form stiff peaks. Stir the yolks into the batter, then fold the batter into the egg whites.

5 Heat a little clarified butter in one large or two small frying pans. Pour the batter into the frying pan. Drain the raisins and sprinkle them, along with the slivered almonds, over the batter. Reduce the heat and fry the pancake for about 10 minutes, or until golden brown underneath. Cover the frying pan if necessary. Carefully turn over the pancake and fry the other side until golden brown.

6 Remove the frying pan from the stove. Using two forks, tear the pancake into bite-sized pieces. Dust generously with icing sugar and return the pan to the stove. Caramelize the sugar over a moderate heat, frequently turning the pancake pieces as you do so.

7 Remove the kaiserschmarrn from the frying pan immediately. Arrange on four plates and dust with icing sugar. Serve with the plum compote.

Crêpes filled with hazelnut cream

Serves 4 · Prep time: 30 minutes · Resting time: 30 minutes

40g (1½oz) melted
 unsalted butter
150g (5½oz) plain flour
pinch of salt
350ml (12fl oz) whole milk
6 eggs
oil, for frying
chocolate-and-hazelnut
 spread (from jar),
 for spreading

1 Leave the melted butter to cool a little. Combine the flour and salt in a bowl. Add the milk and eggs, and whisk to make a thin batter. Stir in the melted butter, cover, and leave to rest for about 30 minutes.

2 Heat a little oil in a frying pan. Pour in a ladleful of batter and tilt the pan to ensure the batter evenly coats the bottom of the frying pan. Fry the crêpe on each side until golden brown. Remove from the frying pan and keep warm. Repeat until the batter is used up – it should produce about 8 very thin crêpes, depending on the size of the frying pan.

3 Spread each of the crêpes with the chocolate-and-hazelnut spread, fold up, and serve immediately.

Tip: Crêpes are perfect for sweet fillings, such as bananas, stewed apple purée, cinnamon sugar, plum compote (see p.124), jam, or icing sugar. They are also delicious with savoury fillings, such as pesto, tomatoes, feta cheese, Emmental cheese, ham, spinach, or creamy wild mushroom stew (see p.89).

Fresh waffles

Serves 4 · Prep time: 45 minutes

250g (9oz) plain flour
1 tsp baking powder
150g (5½oz) melted
 unsalted butter
150g (5½oz) caster sugar
1 tsp freshly grated lemon zest
3 eggs
250ml (9fl oz) sparkling
 mineral water
oil, for frying
icing sugar, for dusting

You will also need
a waffle iron

1 Combine the flour and baking powder in a bowl. Beat the butter, sugar, and lemon zest in a bowl until foamy. Stir in the eggs one at a time. Add the flour mixture and the sparkling water, and combine to make a smooth batter.

2 Turn on the waffle iron. Brush a little oil on the cooking surfaces. For each waffle, pour a small ladleful of batter on the bottom half of the waffle iron. Close the lid and bake the waffle for about 5 minutes until crisp. Remove the waffle. Continue until the batter is used up. Lay out the waffles side by side on a wire rack, dust them with icing sugar, and serve immediately.

Tip: Add a dollop of whipped cream to the freshly baked waffles and serve with fresh fruit, stewed apple purée, plum compote (see p.124), jam, or cinnamon sugar, to taste.

Toffee apples
with hundreds and thousands

Everyone loves to dress up in their prettiest dirndl and smartest pair of lederhosen for Oktoberfest. Even ordinary apples look very festive in their bright red toffee coats.

Makes 12 · Prep time: 45 minutes · Cooling time: 1 hour

12 apples
400g (14oz) caster sugar
100ml (3½fl oz) agave syrup
a few drops of red
  food colouring
100g (3½oz) multicoloured
  hundreds and thousands

You will also need
12 long wooden skewers

1 Wash and thoroughly dry the apples. Pierce each apple from the top through to the bottom with a wooden skewer. Chill the apples for at least 1 hour.

2 In a pan, stir together the sugar, agave syrup, and 150ml (5fl oz) water and cook over a low heat for about 30 minutes until syrupy. Test the syrup by dropping a dribble of it into cold water. If the sugar hardens in the water and can be rolled into a firm ball, the toffee is ready. If not, cook the syrup for another 5 minutes and repeat the test. Add enough food colouring to turn the toffee a deep red and take the pan off the hob.

3 Scatter the hundreds and thousands onto a large plate. Dip each chilled apple into the toffee once or twice, leave to drip briefly, and immediately roll the bottom half of the apple in the sprinkles. Finally, sit the apples on the sprinkles and leave to harden in a dry place for about 15 minutes.

4 Serve the toffee apples as soon as possible – depending on the air humidity, the toffee coating may become sticky again after a few hours.

Tip: To make chocolate-dipped fruit, melt dark, milk, or white chocolate in a bain-marie or in a bowl set over a pan of just-simmering water. Skewer whole fruit such as strawberries or grapes, or pieces of banana, apple, pineapple, or mango, and dip them into the melted chocolate. Sprinkle to taste with chopped nuts or hundreds and thousands, and leave to dry on a cake rack.

Roasted almonds and nuts

Makes 750g (1¾lb) · Prep time: 20 minutes

500g (1lb 2oz) almonds
  and mixed nuts (such as
  hazelnuts, walnuts, pecans,
  and peanuts)
250g (9oz) caster sugar
½ tsp ground cinnamon

1 Line a baking tray with baking parchment. Dry-roast the almonds and mixed nuts in a large frying pan over a low heat, stirring all the time, until you can smell the scent of the roasted nuts.

2 Divide the sugar into thirds. Sprinkle a third of the sugar over the nuts in the pan and wait until the sugar is caramelized. Repeat this step with the second portion of sugar, and again with the last portion. Finally, stir in the cinnamon.

3 Immediately remove the roasted nuts from the pan and spread them out on the lined baking tray. Leave to cool briefly and serve while still warm.

Almond and pistachio nougat

Makes 500g (1lb 2oz) · Prep time: 30 minutes · Drying time: 2 days ·
Keeps for: 3 weeks

3 egg whites
pinch of salt
200g (7oz) caster sugar
1 packet vanilla sugar, or
  1 tsp pure vanilla extract
4 tbsp honey
100g (3½oz) almonds
50g (1¾oz) pistachios
50g (1¾oz) mixed candied
  orange and lemon peel,
  finely diced

1 Put the egg whites and salt in a stainless steel bowl and beat until they form stiff peaks. Drizzle in the sugar and vanilla sugar, or vanilla extract, beating constantly, then add the honey and beat until the mixture is thick.

2 Place the bowl over a pan of simmering water. Beating constantly, heat the mixture to about 70°C (160°F). For best results, check the temperature using a thermometer, such as a sugar thermometer. Then remove the bowl from the simmering water immediately.

3 Stir the almonds, pistachios, and candied peel into the egg whites. Line a deep baking pan or roasting tray with baking parchment and pour in the mixture. Leave to dry for at least 1 day. Then cover the nougat with baking parchment, put a chopping board on top, and weigh down the board with, for example, cans of food. Leave the nougat to rest for at least 1 more day. It should be firm enough to cut, but still sticky.

4 Dip a knife in water and slice the nougat into rectangles or cubes. Serve right away or store in an airtight tin, layered with parchment paper.

Glazed gingerbread
with aromatic spices

This type of gingerbread is called "magenbrot" ("stomach bread"), as it is thought to be good for the digestion. A popular Oktoberfest treat, it is easy to make and keeps well.

Makes about 30 pieces · Prep time: 35 minutes · Baking time: 20 minutes · Resting time: 1 week · Keeps for: 3 weeks

For the dough
250g (9oz) plain flour
250g (9oz) wholemeal
  rye flour
2 tsp baking powder
200g (7oz) caster sugar
1 tsp ground cinnamon
pinch of ground cloves
1 large egg
250ml (9fl oz) whole milk

For the sugar glaze
250g (9oz) caster sugar
1 tbsp cocoa powder

1 Preheat the oven to 180°C (350°F/Gas 4). Line a baking tray with baking parchment. Combine both types of flour, the baking powder, sugar, cinnamon, and cloves. Add the egg and milk, and knead well to make a smooth dough. Shape the dough into three logs about 4cm (1½in) in diameter.

2 Place the dough logs on the baking tray and bake in the middle of the oven for about 20 minutes. Remove from the oven and, while still warm, cut the logs diagonally into slices about 4cm (1½in) thick.

3 To make the sugar glaze, bring the sugar, cocoa powder, and a scant 125ml (4½fl oz) of water to the boil in a pot. Working in batches, dip the rhombus-shaped gingerbread pieces into the glaze and then put them on a cake rack to dry. If you like, dip each a second time. Once the glaze has dried, layer the gingerbread in a tin with a tight-fitting lid and rest for 1 week before serving, to allow the flavours to develop.

Granatsplitter

These mini cakes are an elegant way of using up leftover baked goods such as cakes and cookies. For many Oktoberfest visitors, they are a taste of pure happiness! They are best eaten out of the palm of your hand.

Makes 8 pieces · Prep time: 1 hour · Cooling time: 4 hours 30 minutes

For the dough
50g (1¾oz) cold, unsalted, butter
100g (3½oz) plain flour, plus extra for dusting
25g (1oz) caster sugar
1 large egg yolk

To make the filling and glaze
30g (1oz) cornstarch
1 tbsp cocoa powder
2 tbsp caster sugar
1 packet vanilla sugar or 1 tsp pure vanilla extract
250ml (9fl oz) whole milk
3 tbsp slivered almonds
200g (7oz) leftover cake and cookies
100g (3½oz) good-quality dark chocolate (with a high level of cocoa solids)
250g (9oz) softened unsalted butter
40ml (1½fl oz) rum
coconut flakes, for sprinkling

You will also need
a round pastry cutter, about 6cm (2½in) in diameter

1 To make the dough for the pastry rounds, cut the butter into cubes. Mix together the flour and sugar, then add the butter, egg yolk, and about 3 tablespoons of cold water. Working quickly, knead to make a firm dough. Wrap the dough in cling film and rest in the fridge for about 30 minutes.

2 Preheat the oven to 180°C (350°F/Gas 4). Line a baking tray with baking parchment. Roll out the dough on a floured work surface and cut out 8 circles with the pastry cutter. Place the pastry rounds and the remaining dough cut-offs on the baking tray and bake in the middle of the oven for about 10 minutes, or until golden brown. Remove from the oven and leave to cool.

3 To make the filling, stir together the cornstarch, cocoa powder, sugar, and vanilla sugar or vanilla extract, and half the milk. Bring the remaining milk to the boil. Add the cornstarch mixture to the boiling milk and cook for about 2 minutes, stirring constantly, to make a thick, firm, pudding. Remove from the stove and leave to cool, stirring occasionally to prevent a skin forming.

4 Dry-roast the slivered almonds in a frying pan, stirring constantly, until they are golden brown. Remove from the heat and set aside to cool. Crumble the leftover cake, cookies, and baked pastry remnants. Melt the chocolate gently over a bain-marie (see tip p.128).

5 Beat the butter until foamy. Stir in the pudding, 1 tablespoonful at a time. Add the cake, cookie, and pastry crumbs, slivered almonds, and rum, and stir together to make a creamy mixture. Pour into a freezer bag, snip off one of the corners, and pipe onto the pastry rounds to make a tower shape. Pour the melted chocolate over the cakes and immediately sprinkle with coconut flakes.

6 Refrigerate the cakes for about 4 hours before serving. They taste perfect with a cup of coffee.

Gingerbread hearts
decorated with icing sugar

Simple messages such as "Greetings from Oktoberfest", "I love you", or "Kiss me" are just some of the many gingerbread heart inscriptions you may come across at the fair. These large heart-shaped gingerbread cookies are perfect as gifts, for tucking into yourself, or as Oktoberfest decorations at home!

Makes 4 hearts · Prep time: 2 hours 30 minutes · Chilling time: 8 hours · Baking time: 15 minutes

For the dough
100g (3½oz) unsalted butter
250g (9oz) honey
250g (9oz) light brown sugar
600g (1lb 5oz) plain flour, plus
  extra for dusting
1 tbsp cocoa powder
2 tsp ground cinnamon
1 tsp ground ginger
½ tsp ground allspice
½ tsp ground anise seed
½ tsp ground cardamom
½ tsp ground coriander
¼ tsp ground cloves
¼ tsp grated nutmeg
½ tbsp baking soda
1 large egg

For the icing
2 egg whites
400g (14oz) icing sugar
food colouring in
  various colours

You will also need
1 heart-shaped cardboard
  template, about
  20cm (8in) across
small freezer bag
coloured ribbons (optional)

1 For the dough, combine the butter, honey, and brown sugar in a small pan and bring to the boil, stirring constantly. Then remove from the stove and leave to cool.

2 Combine the flour, cocoa, spices, and baking soda in a bowl. Stir the egg into the butter mixture. Add the butter mixture to the flour, and knead to make a smooth dough. Wrap in cling film and put into the fridge to chill for at least 8 hours.

3 Remove the dough from the fridge and let it come to room temperature, about 1 hour. Preheat the oven to 180°C (350°F/Gas 4). Line two baking trays with baking parchment. Turn out the dough onto a floured work surface and roll out until about 1cm (½in) thick. Using the template, cut out 4 hearts from the dough and place on the baking tray. Bake in the middle of the oven for about 15 minutes, then remove from the oven and leave to cool.

4 To make the icing, beat the egg whites until they form soft peaks. Gradually beat in the sifted icing sugar to make a thick icing. Use the food colouring to make different coloured icing and transfer each coloured icing into a small freezer bag. Snip a small corner off each bag, then use to pipe words and decorations onto the gingerbread hearts. Leave to dry for about 30 minutes.

5 If you like, make two holes in the top of each heart, thread with enough ribbon to hang around your neck, and tie the ends in a knot.

Where, when, what, how:
a brief visitors' guide to the fair

Where can I stay during the fair?

No matter where you decide to stay during Oktoberfest, the number one rule is to plan ahead! Book your hotel room at least a year in advance. To rent an apartment, keep an eye out on the Internet early on. Munich is fully booked during the fair, and the prices go up with demand. Camping is a good alternative if you like to be close to nature and don't need luxury or peace and quiet. The popular city camping ground in München-Thalkirchen, right on the Isar river, is beautifully located but very busy during Oktoberfest. You can do as many Italians do and rent a motorhome for a few days; if you choose this option, it is advisable to rent a space in the dedicated Oktoberfest camping grounds in München-Riem. If you are really lucky, you might have friends in Munich who have a spare bed and are happy to join you for a tour of Oktoberfest.

When should I go to the fair?

You can experience the fair in very different ways at different times. When you might enjoy it most will depend on who you go with and what you plan to do. In general, it is quietest during the week until mid-afternoon. After about 3pm, more and more visitors arrive at the tents, among them many companies with their employees or customers. The party only really gets going after 6pm, when the bands start to play the Oktoberfest hits – until then, things have a more traditional feel.

If you are looking for Bavarian "gemütlichkeit" (coziness and friendliness), you won't find it on a Saturday. On this day, the huge crowds barely make any progress between one ride and the next, and often the tents are already closed early in the morning due to overcrowding. Avoid Saturdays if at all possible, especially if you are a first-time visitor, as you may get the wrong impression and be disappointed. Saturdays on the fairgrounds are generally unsuitable for families with children – in fact, buggies are not permitted in the fairgrounds at all on these days.

How can I reserve a table?

Even Munich residents dream of reserving a table at the fair! Unfortunately, simply picking up the phone and booking ahead, as you would do with a restaurant, does not work. Your best bet is to contact your chosen festival tent landlord six to eight months before the fair, either by letter, by fax, or by online form. Information about how to reserve a table can be found on the festival tent's website. Without exception, you will need ten people to make a reservation – this is the number of guests who fit around a beer table. And then you will need to be patient – and lucky: there is no reservation guarantee. If you have been successful, a letter of confirmation – giving the date, time, and table number – will be sent out to you from around the end of February. Remember that reservations are limited to a specific time slot, so if you have been lucky enough to bag a table reservation, it is absolutely essential that you and your party turn up on time for your designated slot.

How do I get to the fair and back?

Two-thirds of all visitors travel to the fair by S-Bahn or U-Bahn. You have a choice of 4 train stations. The main station for the fair, Theresienwiese, is often overcrowded. Alternatively, get off at S-Bahn station Hackerbrücke or U-Bahn stations Goetheplatz or Poccistraße. From these stations, it takes no more than ten minutes to walk to the nearest fairground entrance. Taxis and privately-owned rickshaws are also popular. If you are really only going to drink one "Radler" or shandy, come by bicycle, which can be conveniently parked right in front of the fairgrounds. Taking the car to get there and back, however, is not a good idea. The police carry out many more traffic controls during Oktoberfest – plus, you are unlikely to be able to find a parking spot. A good option for many is to go to the fair by U-Bahn and return home by taxi. This way, you can avoid the overcrowded stations on your way home.

Is Bavarian traditional costume really mandatory?
The answer is "yes and no." A proper traditional outfit can significantly increase the fun factor while giving tradition a nod, too. But before you spend money in some dubious store near the main train station on (artificial) leather shorts "made in China," or on an ill-fitting, cheap dirndl that won't survive the first evening, rest assured: regular clothes are fine, too! The main thing is to be comfortable and have a good time.

Where is the best place to watch the Grand Entry and the Costume and Riflemen's Procession?
Both parade routes go through the city centre. The Grand Entry of the Oktoberfest Landlords and Breweries on Saturday takes a shorter route along Sonnenstraße and Schwanthalerstraße to the fairgrounds. The Costume and Riflemen's Procession, which lasts about three hours, begins on Maximilianstraße at the Isar river, continues past the Residenz and Odeonsplatz, along Brienner Straße to Sonnenstraße and then on to the fairgrounds,

so these roads are closed to traffic for the parade. If you want to watch the parade, remember: he or she who sits, pays! Seating stands are set up along the entire route. Tickets can be purchased in advance (for example from Munich Ticket) at a cost of around €35 (£25). Standing room is free, but you need to be at your chosen spot early, wear comfortable shoes, and, above all, have good stamina.

Where can I carry on celebrating in Oktoberfest style after the tents have closed?
The tents close at 11.30pm, except for the Weinzelt tent and Käferl's gourmet tent, where you can celebrate until 1am. Once the curfew has passed, Oktoberfest closes for the day. After-parties have been trendy in Munich for several years. They are held across the city – although most are not too far from the fairgrounds – in bars, pubs, clubs, and sometimes also in spaces not usually used as party venues, until 3am or later. Seasoned fairgoers often prefer to go straight home and be reasonably fit to go back for another round the next day. After all, the fair lasts for only 16 days, whereas the clubs are open all year. On the other hand, if you are enjoying your holiday, you might as well make the most out of it. At the end of the day, it's up to you!

A guide to beer-tent Bavarian

Oktoberfest is a Bavarian festival – you will definitely meet some locals who speak in the Bavarian dialect – and being able to communicate effectively is important. So you don't miss out in the sociable atmosphere of the tents, help is at hand. This glossary of phrases will prepare you for some standard situations at Oktoberfest. It will help you understand compliments, respond appropriately, and overcome any tricky situations. Along with the often heard "Oans, zwoa, gsuffa!" ("One, two, bottoms up!"), the following expressions will come in handy:

In the beer tent

A Mass und ein Hendl, biddschön	"A mass (litre) of beer and half a roast chicken, please"
(I kriagat) no oane	"I'd like another beer"
Oane geht no	"I can handle one more mass (at least, I think so)"
Kracherl	Carbonated lemon soda
Mongtratzerl	A small appetizer. Also often used to complain about a portion that is too small ("Des war ja nur a Mongtratzerl" – "That was just a mongtratzerl")
Stamperl	A schnapps glass or a glass of schnapps (i.e. the contents)
I konn nimma	"I'm (more than) full"
lack	Stale, no longer sparkling (beer, sodas)
Schwoam mas obi!	"Let's empty our mugs!" Also, "Let's have a beer, instead of arguing!"
Noagerl	A little bit of beer left at the bottom of the beer mug
Noagerlzuzler	Someone who nurses his or her beer and doesn't order a fresh one
Sauf di zamm!	"Drink up!"

Starting and ending a conversation

Servus/Griaß di	Used when greeting someone
Servus/Griaßts eich	Used when greeting several/many people
Is do no frei?	"Is this seat free?"
Hock di hera, rutsch ma zamm	"We'll make room for you and move a bit closer together"
Hock di hera, samma mera	Popular jocular saying that means the same as above
fei	A difficult-to-translate phatic expression generally used to strengthen a statement ("Des beer is fei guat" means "This beer is actually really good")
Mei, ham mir a Gaudi!	"We're having fun here, aren't we!"
Wos bleast denn so?	"You don't need to shout, I can hear you very well"
Eam/sie schaug oo!	Depending on the situation, either an admiring or a disrespectful comment about what someone has just said or done ("Eam" for males, "Sie" for females)

Interpersonal encounters

Gschpusi	Male or female companion, friend, lover, or mistress
Deandl	This usually doesn't refer to a dirndl dress, but a young girl
obandln	Flirting, chatting up members of the opposite sex
I mog di	"I find you attractive, and would like to get to know you better"
Du bist a ganz a scheena Fega	A compliment paid to a (young) lady you actually don't want to get to know better, although she is attractive
Deaf i dia a Busserl gebm?	"May I kiss you?" (a busserl is a short kiss on the cheek or mouth)
Hoiz vo da Hüttn	An ample dirndl cleavage
gwampert	Fat, with a large stomach
Grischperl	A weedy man
Bazi	Swindler, a scheming fellow
Gschaftlhuaba	Someone who is very full of themselves
Preiß	A visitor who speaks high German
Saupreiß	A disagreeable visitor who speaks high German
oide Zausl	A term for an older man who behaves in an undignified way
oide Dackl	A term for an older man with an excessive interest in females
Spinatwachtl	A swear word for an older, slightly eccentric lady
bleede Hena	A mild swear word for a female who has aroused disapproval
Schaug, dassd weida kimmst/ Geh, schleich di!	"You'd better leave (slither off) right away"
Mogsd a Schelln/Watschn/Fotzn?	"I'm going to clobber you one in a minute!"
Nimm deine Bratzn (do) weg!	"You are getting a bit too close/get off!"
Sei hoid ned so zwieda!	"Why are you so unfriendly?"

In front of and behind the tent, and on the way home

Ziegarn	A cigar, smoked behind the tent
Drah ma no a Rundn	"Let's take another stroll over the fairgrounds"
Guadln	Sweets
Heb di (bei mia) ei!	"Hold on to my arm!" (in cases where someone is the worse for wear after leaving the tent)
I wui hoam	"I want to go home"
Mia is ned guad/I muaß speibm/ Mia draat si ois	"I'm feeling unwell/I'll be sick/I'm dizzy"
I geh amoi aufs Haisl!	"I'm going for a quick visit to the toilets"
wuid biesln	Not seeking out the proper sanitary facilities to urinate
Pfiat di/eana!	"Bye bye!"
Wia schaugts aus, seng ma uns wieda?	"Will we be seeing each other again?"

Index

Recipe index

Subject index

Acknowledgments

Jasmin Blanda: Thank you for the super food styling assistance and your work as a hand model.
Team Block K: Thank you to the world's best service team – Martina Bendig, Daniela Geisenberger, Susanne Haas, Sonja Herpich, Eva Ludwig and Andrea Wellmann-Burk – in the Hofbräu tent.
DK: Thank you for making this book a reality.
Stefan Hempl and Hofbräu Munich: Thank you for the generous support with beer, props, and plenty of room for taking photographs.
Rudl Herpich: Thank you, you clever Bavarian man and first-class model.
Marianne Kranz: Thank you for the fabulous dirndl dresses. www.exklusive-tracht.de
Eva Probst: Thank you for the excellent Bavarian sausages and the absolutely top-quality meat. www.metzgerei-probst.de
Michaela Schifferl and Tobias Martl: Thank you for decorating all those gingerbread hearts for the cover photo. www.lebkuchen-herzl.de
Feline Skowronek: Thank you to our favourite model.
Brigitte Sporrer: Thank you for the wonderful photographs in this book.
The Steinberg family: Thank you for 20 shared years at the fair.
Martin Widmann and HB Logistik: Thank you for the beautiful decommissioned beer tables for the photographs. www.schanktec.de
Julia Skowronek, trained cook, Münchner by choice, food stylist, and author, lives in Munich. The Bavarian cuisine and the "Wiesn" are particularly close to her heart. She has also worked for 20 years as a waiter in the Hofbräu tent during the Oktoberfest.

Recipes and food styling Julia Skowronek
Additional text by Katja Treu
Photographer Brigitte Sporrer
Editor Petra Teetz
Designer and illustrator Silke Klemt

DK Germany
Publishing Director Monika Schlitzer
Project Editor Sarah Fischer
Production Director Dorothee Whittaker
Producer Sophie Schiela
Production Co-ordinator Katharina Dürmeier
Translation Barbara Hopkinson

DK UK
Project Editor Anna-Selina Sander
Editor Bob Bridle
Managing Editor Dawn Henderson
Managing Art Editor Christine Keilty
Senior Pre-Production Producer Tony Phipps
Senior Producer Stephanie McConnell
Senior Jacket Creative Nicola Powling
Jacket Co-ordinator Francesca Young
Jacket Design Assistant Amy Keast

First published in Great Britain in 2015 by
Dorling Kindersley Limited
80 Strand, London, WC2R 0RL

Copyright © 2015
Dorling Kindersley Limited
A Penguin Random House Company

2 4 6 8 10 9 7 5 3 1
001–284986–Aug/2015

A CIP catalogue record for this book is available from the British Library.
ISBN: 978-0-2412-1681-1

Printed and bound in Hong Kong

All images © Dorling Kindersley Limited
For further information see: www.dkimages.com

A WORLD OF IDEAS:
SEE ALL THERE IS TO KNOW

NOTE: The author and publisher advocate sustainable food choices, and every effort has been made to include only sustainable foods in this book. Food sustainability is, however, a shifting landscape, and so we encourage readers to keep up to date with advice on this subject, so that they are equipped to make their own ethical choices.